POEMS ON
THE UNDERGROUND

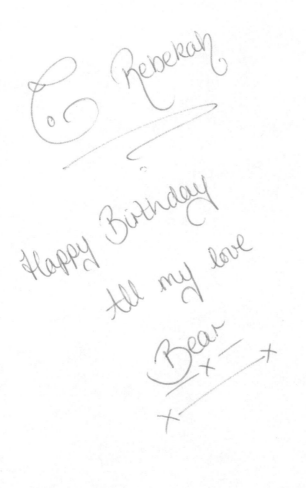

To Rebekah

Happy Birthday

All my love

Bear

x — x

x

POEMS
ON THE
UNDERGROUND

FOURTH EDITION

edited by
Gerard Benson
Judith Chernaik
Cicely Herbert

CASSELL

Cassell Publishers Limited
Villiers House, 41/47 Strand
London WC2N 5JE

100 Poems on the Underground
first published 1991
Poems on the Underground Illustrated Edition
first published 1992
Poems on the Underground New and Extended Edition
first published 1993
Fourth Edition first published 1994

British Library Cataloguing in Publication Data
A catalogue record for this book is available from the British Library

ISBN 0–304–34449–4

Distributed in Australia by
Capricorn Link (Australia) Pty Ltd
2/13 Carrington Road
Castle Hill, NSW 2154

Distributed in the United States by
Sterling Publishing Co, Inc.
387 Park Avenue South, New York, NY 10016–8810

Typeset in Monophoto Meridien by
August Filmsetting, Haydock, St Helens

Printed and bound in Great Britain by
Mackays of Chatham PLC, Chatham, Kent

CONTENTS

LIST OF ILLUSTRATIONS

INTRODUCTION

ANYONE who suffers from an addiction to reading cereal box tops or bus tickets will understand the special appeal of 'Poems on the Underground'. The programme began as an idea shared among a few friends: how pleasant it would be, we thought, to read a few lines by one's favourite poet on the Tube, instead of advertisements for trouser presses or temps. We were Londoners by birth or adoption, habitual users of public transport, lovers of poetry. We shared the conviction that poetry is a popular, living art, and that the pleasures of rhythm and rhyme are part of common life. The Underground, also an inescapable part of our common life, had large numbers of empty advertising spaces. It seemed an entirely reasonable idea to propose filling the blank grey slots with poems, for the entertainment of the travelling public.

London Underground was surprisingly responsive to our suggestion that they provide unlet spaces free for this civic purpose. They agreed that if we could raise money to pay a modest charge for five hundred spaces, they would match the number. With an Arts Council grant from the Compton Poetry Fund, set up 'for the wider dissemination of poetry', and generous support from the publishers Faber and Faber, who produced the posters for the first two years, and Oxford University Press, who provided matching funds, we presented the first group of poems to an unsuspecting public.

On Wednesday, 29 January 1986, 'Poems on the Underground' was officially launched at Aldwych, a station usually closed between rush hours, and often used for filming movies about the Second World War. Many of those who descended to the Underground platform that rain-drenched morning might have had in mind the journey made to the infernal regions by Orpheus in search of Eurydice. Ordinary signs – TICKETS AND TRAINS, THIS WAY DOWN, STAND CLEAR, DOORS CLOSING – assume a special significance when such a setting is taken over by poets and their friends. Official party fare was coffee and doughnuts, but wine flowed too, and when the train bearing its consignment of poems arrived, twenty minutes late, we all climbed aboard, pursued by representatives of the press, radio and television. Within minutes the carriages were alive to the sounds of happy poets declaiming verse by Shelley, Burns and, of course, by themselves.

When we began to scatter poems about in public, we had no idea how people would respond; it was all a bit reminiscent of the lovesick youth in the Forest of Arden, hanging 'odes upon hawthorns and elegies on brambles'. Not that the London Underground is anything like the Forest of Arden; on the contrary, it is the ultimate expression of the modern urban working world. But poetry thrives on paradox, and the poems seemed to take on new and surprising life when they were removed from books and set amongst the adverts. Commuters enjoyed the idea of reading Keats's 'Much have I travell'd in the realms of gold' on a crowded Central Line train, or trying to memorise a sonnet between Leicester Square and Hammersmith. Just as we had hoped, the poems provided relief, caused smiles, offered refreshment to the soul – and all in a place where one would least expect to find anything remotely poetic.

The truth, as we soon discovered, is that England is a nation of poetry-lovers. Hundreds of people wrote in with queries about particular poems, suggestions of their own, and comments; many letters just said, in effect, 'Thank you, whoever you are, for the poems.' Three years after our launch, London Underground agreed to provide all spaces free and to quadruple the number, in theory providing at least one poem to each train carriage, and to pay production costs as well. Posters go to British Council libraries throughout the world, and the London Transport Museum maintains a subscription list, mainly for schools and libraries, but also for hospitals, community centres and prisons. We are set to continue indefinitely, and there seems no possibility of running out of poems, either from the past or by contemporary poets.

From the start, we have tried to offer as wide a variety of tone and subject matter as possible, to share our own favourites and our special discoveries, but also to present new voices. At least two poems out of each group of five (occasionally six) are by living poets. We have taken material from the earliest times to the present, and we have made a point of including poets from English-speaking countries throughout the world. A few translations are also included, and 'Anon.' features largely, in songs and riddles, nursery rhymes and broadsheet ballads.

We have kept a special place for London poems, and for poets who had close associations with London – Donne, Milton, Blake and Keats, among others – though some of the most celebrated London poems (like 'To the City of London', by the Scottish poet William Dunbar, and Wordsworth's 'Composed Upon West-minster Bridge') were written by poets as they were passing through. Of London poems in our collection by contemporary writers, one is by the New Zealand-born poet Fleur Adcock, another by the Guyanese poet Grace Nichols. Then again, A. E. Housman wrote *A Shropshire Lad* when he was working every day at the Chancery Lane Patent Office; and we have assumed that the imagination is free to wander where it will. What we have listened for is the individual voice, and we have tried to offer poems in which the poet's voice speaks directly to the modern reader about the common themes of poetry through the ages.

The great subjects are well represented here: love, death, war, the natural world, time, memory. But these are not the only themes of poetry, nor is the high-flown the only mode. There is also a fine tradition of comic verse, and in amongst the passion and nostalgia we placed a few banana skins in the form of light, humorous and quirky verse. We have included writers of comic nonsense like Edward Lear, Spike Milligan and Wendy Cope; there are also pieces in a witty, conversational vein by poets ranging from Michael Drayton and William Carlos Williams to Stevie Smith and Liz Lochhead. Some light or funny verse was chosen with children in mind, but we found that these poems often appealed as much to adults as to children; Roger McGough's 'The Leader' found its way into a number of boardrooms and political party headquarters.

This anthology has come about in response to public interest in the programme, and in particular poems that appeared briefly on the Tube and then vanished from sight, leaving only a memory of a single line or image. They are all here (with one substitution) in the order in which they appeared on the Tube, in groups of five or six. Many of the poems will be familiar to readers; others are fairly obscure and hard to find without special library resources; some are unique to this volume. We hope that the collection as a whole will appeal not only to addicted poetry-lovers but also to readers who are coming to poetry for the first time.

Gerard Benson, Judith Chernaik, Cicely Herbert
London, 1991

INTRODUCTION TO THE
FOURTH EDITION

IN THE fourth edition of *Poems on the Underground*, we include forty-five poems which have been displayed on Underground trains during the past three years. Fifteen of these were included in the *Illustrated Edition* (1992), which also includes colour reproductions of twenty-four historic Underground posters. Another fifteen were included in the New and Extended Edition (1993).

Poems on the Underground has now been in existence for nine years and has spawned a number of associated projects: a 12-hour Remembrance Day reading at St James's Church, Piccadilly, with over 90 poets participating; poetry workshops on Westminster Bridge and Waterloo Bridge; children's workshops at the London Transport Museum and in London primary schools. A grant from the Calouste Gulbenkian Foundation twice enabled us to fill every advertising space in a Circle Line train carriage with poems written by schoolchildren, with a third display of children's poems held on station platforms of the District Line in 1993. We have given annual readings at the British Library, drawing on the great Library collections, as part of the Stefan Zweig Series. Poems featured on the Tube have been read on local and national radio and on the BBC World Service, which has broadcast the Tube poems throughout the world. Similar projects have sprung up elsewhere in Britain and abroad, with poems riding public transport systems in Bristol, Newcastle and West Yorkshire, Dublin, Stuttgart and Würzburg, and (most recently) in New York City, Paris, Stockholm, Sydney and Melbourne.

Soon after the New York City programme was launched, we suggested an exchange of poems between the two great public transit systems, as a modest contribution to cross-cultural understanding. In May 1994, 4,000 copies of the sixteenth-century

English song 'Western Wind', with the original British Library manuscript, went on display in New York City trains and buses. At the same time, riders of London's Underground were offered the first section of 'Crossing Brooklyn Ferry' by that most American of poets, Walt Whitman. The exchange was marked by a poetry reading at Grand Central Station, recently restored to its early splendour, with a return engagement at the London Transport Museum. A similar exchange is in prospect with Stockholm for 1995.

We have also expanded into new territory by commissioning several poets featured on the Underground to write poems for Saint-Saëns' 'Carnival of the Animals'. And we recently learned that the composer Thea Musgrave has set six of the Underground poems for unaccompanied choir, offering the poems in yet another guise to new audiences.

We continue to receive support, encouragement and suggestions for poems from a large and generous readership, to whom we say: long may poetry flourish, on the Underground, on the printed page, and in the hearts and minds of the people.

G.B., J.C., C.H. London, 1994

ACKNOWLEDGEMENTS

The editors and publisher gratefully acknowledge permission to reproduce the following copyright poems in this book:

Fleur Adcock: 'Immigrant' from *Selected Poems* (1983), © Fleur Adcock 1983. Reprinted by permission of Oxford University Press.

Moniza Alvi: 'Arrival 1946' from *The Country at my Shoulder* (1993) © Moniza Alvi 1993. Reprinted by permission of Oxford University Press.

Maya Angelou: 'Come. And Be My Baby' from *Just Give Me A Cool Drink of Water 'Fore I Diiie*, © Maya Angelou 1971. Reprinted by permission of Virago Press.

W. H. Auden: Song ('Stop all the clocks, cut off the telephone') and 'If I could tell you' from *Collected Poems* by W. H. Auden, © W. H. Auden 1968. Reprinted by permission of Faber and Faber.

Bei Dao: 'A Picture' from *Old Snow*, Anvil, © Bei Dao 1990. Reprinted by permission of David Higham Associates.

Gerard Benson: 'The Coming of Grendel' from *Beowulf*, and 'Old English Riddle', © Gerard Benson 1988 and 1990. Reprinted by permission of the author.

Oliver Bernard, translator: 'Letter to André Billy. 9 April 1915' from Guillaume Apollinaire, *Selected Poems* (1986), translation © Oliver Bernard 1986. Reprinted by permission of Anvil Press.

James Berry: 'Benediction' from *Chain of Days* (1985), © James Berry 1985. Reprinted by permission of Oxford University Press.

Sujata Bhatt: 'Love in a Bathtub' from *Monkey Fires*, © Sujata Bhatt 1991. Reprinted by permission of Carcanet Press.

Elizabeth Bishop: 'One Art' from *Complete Poems 1927–1979*, © Alice Helen Methfessel 1983. Reprinted by permission of Farrar, Straus and Giroux.

Valerie Bloom: 'Sun a-shine, rain a-fall' from *Duppy Jamboree* (1992) © Cambridge University Press. Reprinted by permission of Cambridge University Press.

Eavan Boland: 'The Emigrant Irish', from *Selected Poems* © Eavan Boland 1986. Reprinted by permission of Carcanet Press.

Edward Kamau Brathwaite: 'Mmenson' from *The Arrivants* (1973), © Edward Kamau Brathwaite 1973. Reprinted by permission of Oxford University Press.

Charles Causley: 'I Saw a Jolly Hunter' from *Figgie Hobbin* © Charles Causley 1970. Reprinted by permission of Macmillan Publishers and David Higham Associates.

Eiléan Ní Chuilleanáin: 'Swineherd' from *The Second Voyage* © Eiléan Ní Chuilleanáin 1986. Reprinted by permission of Gallery Books.

Gillian Clarke: 'Taid's Grave' from *Selected Poems*, © Gillian Clarke 1985. Reprinted by permission of Carcanet Press.

THE POEMS

Up in the Morning Early

Cauld blaws the wind frae east to west,
　The drift is driving sairly;
Sae loud and shrill's I hear the blast,
　I'm sure it's winter fairly.

CHORUS: Up in the morning's no for me,
　Up in the morning early;
When a' the hills are cover'd wi' snaw,
　I'm sure it's winter fairly.

The birds sit chittering in the thorn,
　A' day they fare but sparely;
And lang's the night frae e'en to morn,
　I'm sure it's winter fairly.

CHORUS: Up in the morning's no for me,
　Up in the morning early;
When a' the hills are cover'd wi' snaw,
　I'm sure it's winter fairly.

ROBERT BURNS (1759–96)

Ozymandias

I met a traveller from an antique land
Who said: Two vast and trunkless legs of stone
Stand in the desert... Near them, on the sand,
Half sunk, a shattered visage lies, whose frown,
And wrinkled lip, and sneer of cold command,
Tell that its sculptor well those passions read
Which yet survive, stamped on these lifeless things,
The hand that mocked them and the heart that fed;
And on the pedestal these words appear:
"My name is OZYMANDIAS, king of kings:
Look on my works, ye Mighty, and despair!"
Nothing beside remains. Round the decay
Of that colossal wreck, boundless and bare
The lone and level sands stretch far away.

PERCY BYSSHE SHELLEY (1792–1822)

This Is Just to Say

I have eaten
the plums
that were in
the icebox

and which
you were probably
saving
for breakfast

Forgive me
they were delicious
so sweet
and so cold

WILLIAM CARLOS WILLIAMS (1883–1963)

The Railway Children

When we climbed the slopes of the cutting
We were eye-level with the white cups
Of the telegraph poles and the sizzling wires.

Like lovely freehand they curved for miles
East and miles west beyond us, sagging
Under their burden of swallows.

We were small and thought we knew nothing
Worth knowing. We thought words travelled the wires
In the shiny pouches of raindrops,

Each one seeded full with the light
Of the sky, the gleam of the lines, and ourselves
So infinitesimally scaled

We could stream through the eye of a needle.

SEAMUS HEANEY (b. 1939)

Like a Beacon

In London
every now and then
I get this craving
for my mother's food
I leave art galleries
in search of plantains
saltfish/sweet potatoes

I need this link

I need this touch
of home
swinging my bag
like a beacon
against the cold

GRACE NICHOLS (b. 1950)

Sonnet 29

When in disgrace with Fortune and men's eyes,
I all alone beweep my outcast state,
And trouble deaf heaven with my bootless cries,
And look upon myself and curse my fate,
Wishing me like to one more rich in hope,
Featured like him, like him with friends possessed,
Desiring this man's art, and that man's scope,
With what I most enjoy contented least,
Yet in these thoughts myself almost despising,
Haply I think on thee, and then my state
(Like to the lark at break of day arising
From sullen earth) sings hymns at heaven's gate,
    For thy sweet love remembered such wealth brings,
    That then I scorn to change my state with kings.

WILLIAM SHAKESPEARE (1564–1616)

Her Anxiety

Earth in beauty dressed
Awaits returning spring.
All true love must die,
Alter at the best
Into some lesser thing.
Prove that I lie.

Such body lovers have,
Such exacting breath,
That they touch or sigh.
Every touch they give,
Love is nearer death.
Prove that I lie.

W. B. YEATS (1865–1939)

Lady 'Rogue' Singleton

Come, wed me, Lady Singleton,
And we will have a baby soon
And we will live in Edmonton
Where all the friendly people run.

I could never make you happy, darling,
Or give you the baby you want,
I would always very much rather, dear,
Live in a tent.

I am not a cold woman, Henry,
But I do not feel for you,
What I feel for the elephants and the miasmas
And the general view.

STEVIE SMITH (1902–71)

The Trees

The trees are coming into leaf
Like something almost being said;
The recent buds relax and spread,
Their greenness is a kind of grief.

Is it that they are born again
And we grow old? No, they die too.
Their yearly trick of looking new
Is written down in rings of grain.

Yet still the unresting castles thresh
In fullgrown thickness every May.
Last year is dead, they seem to say,
Begin afresh, afresh, afresh.

PHILIP LARKIN (1922–85)

Benediction

Thanks to the ear
that someone may hear

Thanks to seeing
that someone may see

Thanks to feeling
that someone may feel

Thanks to touch
that one may be touched

Thanks to flowering of white moon
and spreading shawl of black night
holding villages and cities together

JAMES BERRY (b. 1924)

The Sick Rose

O Rose thou art sick.
The invisible worm
That flies in the night
In the howling storm,

Has found out thy bed
Of crimson joy:
And his dark secret love
Does thy life destroy.

WILLIAM BLAKE (1757–1827)

'Much Madness is divinest Sense'

Much Madness is divinest Sense –
To a discerning Eye –
Much Sense – the starkest Madness –
'Tis the Majority
In this, as All, prevail –
Assent – and you are sane –
Demur – you're straightway dangerous –
And handled with a Chain –

EMILY DICKINSON (1830–86)

At Lord's

It is little I repair to the matches of the Southron folk,
   Though my own red roses there may blow;
It is little I repair to the matches of the Southron folk,
   Though the red roses crest the caps, I know.
For the field is full of shades as I near the shadowy coast,
And a ghostly batsman plays to the bowling of a ghost,
And I look through my tears on a soundless-clapping host
   As the run-stealers flicker to and fro,
      To and fro: –
O my Hornby and my Barlow long ago!

FRANCIS THOMPSON (1859–1907)

Rainforest

The forest drips and glows with green.
The tree-frog croaks his far-off song.
His voice is stillness, moss and rain
drunk from the forest ages long.

We cannot understand that call
unless we move into his dream,
where all is one and one is all
and frog and python are the same.

We with our quick dividing eyes
measure, distinguish and are gone.
The forest burns, the tree-frog dies,
yet one is all and all are one.

JUDITH WRIGHT (b. 1915)

Encounter at St. Martin's

I tell a wanderer's tale, the same
I began long ago, a boy in a barn,
I am always lost in it. The place
is always strange to me. In my pocket

the wrong money or none, the wrong paper,
maps of another town, the phrase book
for yesterday's language, just a ticket
to the next station, and my instructions.

In the lobby of the Banco Bilbao
a dark woman will slip me a key, a package,
the name of a hotel, a numbered account,
the first letters of an unknown alphabet.

KEN SMITH (b. 1938)

'Western wind when wilt thou blow'

Western wind when wilt thou blow
the small rain down can rain
Christ if my love were in my arms
and I in my bed again

ANON. (early 16th century)

Westron wynde when wilt thou blow   Musical setting in a tenor part-book, dating from the early sixteenth century, which provides the only known source of this famous lyric. BL Royal MS, Appendix 58, f.5. By permission of The British Library Board.

Composed upon Westminster Bridge, September 3, 1802

Earth has not anything to show more fair:
Dull would he be of soul who could pass by
A sight so touching in its majesty:
This City now doth like a garment wear
The beauty of the morning; silent, bare,
Ships, towers, domes, theatres, and temples lie
Open unto the fields, and to the sky;
All bright and glittering in the smokeless air.
Never did sun more beautifully steep
In his first splendour valley, rock, or hill;
Ne'er saw I, never felt, a calm so deep!
The river glideth at his own sweet will:
Dear God! the very houses seem asleep;
And all that mighty heart is lying still!

WILLIAM WORDSWORTH (1770–1850)

Everyone Sang

Everyone suddenly burst out singing;
And I was filled with such delight
As prisoned birds must find in freedom,
Winging wildly across the white
Orchards and dark-green fields; on – on – and out of sight.

Everyone's voice was suddenly lifted;
And beauty came like the setting sun:
My heart was shaken with tears; and horror
Drifted away . . . O, but Everyone
Was a bird; and the song was wordless; the singing will never
   be done.

April 1919

SIEGFRIED SASSOON (1886–1967)

The Loch Ness Monster's Song

Sssnnnwhufffll?
Hnwhuffl hhnnwfl hnfl hfl?
Gdroblboblhobngbl gbl gl g g g g glbgl.
Drublhaflablhaflubhafgabhaflhafl fl fl –
gm grawwwww grf grawf awfgm graw gm.
Hovoplodok-doplodovok-plovodokot-doplodokosh?
Splgraw fok fok splgrafhatchgabrlgabrl fok splfok!
Zgra kra gka fok!
Grof grawff gahf?
Gombl mbl bl –
blm plm,
blm plm,
blm plm,
blp.

EDWIN MORGAN (b. 1920)

Living

The fire in leaf and grass
so green it seems
each summer the last summer.

The wind blowing, the leaves
shivering in the sun,
each day the last day.

A red salamander
so cold and so
easy to catch, dreamily

moves his delicate feet
and long tail. I hold
my hand open for him to go.

Each minute the last minute.

DENISE LEVERTOV (b. 1923)

Holy Sonnet

Death be not proud, though some have called thee
Mighty and dreadful, for thou art not so;
For those whom thou think'st thou dost overthrow
Die not, poor death, nor yet canst thou kill me.
From rest and sleep, which but thy pictures be,
Much pleasure, then from thee much more must flow;
And soonest our best men with thee do go,
Rest of their bones, and souls' delivery.
Thou art slave to Fate, chance, kings, and desperate men,
And dost with poison, war, and sickness dwell,
And poppy or charms can make us sleep as well,
And better than thy stroke; why swell'st thou then?
One short sleep past, we wake eternally,
And death shall be no more, Death thou shalt die.

JOHN DONNE (1572–1631)

'Trail all your pikes'

Trail all your pikes, dispirit every drum,
March in a slow procession from afar,
Ye silent, ye dejected men of war!
Be still the hautboys, and the flute be dumb!
Display no more, in vain, the lofty banner.
For see! where on the bier before ye lies
The pale, the fall'n, th'untimely sacrifice
To your mistaken shrine, to your false idol Honour!

from ALL IS VANITY

ANNE FINCH, Countess of Winchilsea (1661–1720)

Alas, Alack!

Ann, Ann!
    Come! quick as you can!
There's a fish that *talks*
    In the frying-pan.
Out of the fat,
    As clear as glass,
He put up his mouth
    And moaned 'Alas!'
Oh, most mournful,
    'Alas, alack!'
Then turned to his sizzling,
    And sank him back.

WALTER DE LA MARE (1873–1956)

Alas, Alack!   Drawing by W. Heath Robinson, © The Estate of
Mrs J. C. Robinson. By permission of Laurence Pollinger.

Immigrant

November '63: eight months in London.
I pause on the low bridge to watch the pelicans:
they float swanlike, arching their white necks
over only slightly ruffled bundles of wings,
burying awkward beaks in the lake's water.

I clench cold fists in my Marks and Spencer's jacket
and secretly test my accent once again:
St James's Park; St James's Park; St James's Park.

FLEUR ADCOCK (b. 1934)

I Am Becoming My Mother

Yellow/brown woman
fingers smelling always of onions

My mother raises rare blooms
and waters them with tea
her birth waters sang like rivers
my mother is now me

My mother had a linen dress
the colour of the sky
and stored lace and damask
tablecloths
to pull shame out of her eye.

I am becoming my mother
brown/yellow woman
fingers smelling always of onions.

LORNA GOODISON (b. 1947)

'Tagus farewell'

Tagus farewell, that westward with thy streams
Turns up the grains of gold already tried:
With spur and sail for I go seek the Thames
Gainward the sun that showeth her wealthy pride
And to the town which Brutus sought by dreams
Like bended moon doth lend her lusty side.
My king, my country, alone for whom I live,
Of mighty love the wings for this me give.

SIR THOMAS WYATT (1503–42)

'**Tagus farewell**'   A rare example of a poem in the author's hand, in a
handsome leatherbound notebook he kept from 1537 to 1542, which contains
over one hundred poems by Wyatt and several by the Earl of Surrey, most of
them in the hand of an amanuensis. The notebook was also used for drafts of
letters and mathematical computations over a period of one hundred years.
BL Egerton 2711, f.69. By permission of The British Library Board.

Snow

In the gloom of whiteness,
In the great silence of snow,
A child was sighing
And bitterly saying: 'Oh,
They have killed a white bird up there on her nest,
The down is fluttering from her breast!'
And still it fell through that dusky brightness
On the child crying for the bird of the snow.

EDWARD THOMAS (1878–1917)

Endymion Book 1ˢᵗ

A thing of beauty is a joy for ever:
Its loveliness increases; it will never
Pass into nothingness; but still will keep
a Bower quiet for us, and a sleep
Full of sweet dreams, and health, and quiet breathing
Therefore, on every morrow, are we wreathing
A flowery band to bind us to the earth,
Spite of Despondence, of the inhuman dearth
Of noble natures, of the gloomy days,
Of all the unhealthy and oer-darkened ways
Made for our searching: yes, in spite of all
Some shape of beauty moves away the Pall
From our dark spirits. ~~and before we shawm~~
~~likes glitter on the ~~~~~~

Endymion   The opening lines of the autograph fair copy, with Keats's corrections.
MA 208. By permission of The Pierpont Morgan Library, New York.

Lines *from* Endymion

A thing of beauty is a joy for ever:
Its loveliness increases; it will never
Pass into nothingness; but still will keep
A bower quiet for us, and a sleep
Full of sweet dreams, and health, and quiet breathing.
Therefore, on every morrow, are we wreathing
A flowery band to bind us to the earth,
Spite of despondence, of the inhuman dearth
Of noble natures, of the gloomy days,
Of all the unhealthy and o'er-darkened ways
Made for our searching: yes, in spite of all,
Some shape of beauty moves away the pall
From our dark spirits.

JOHN KEATS (1795–1821)

Celia Celia

When I am sad and weary
When I think all hope has gone
When I walk along High Holborn
I think of you with nothing on

ADRIAN MITCHELL (b. 1932)

Goodbye

He breathed in air, he breathed out light.
Charlie Parker was my delight.

ADRIAN MITCHELL

Ragwort

They won't let railways alone, those yellow flowers.
They're that remorseless joy of dereliction
darkest banks exhale like vivid breath
as bricks divide to let them root between.
How every falling place concocts their smile,
taking what's left and making a song of it.

ANNE STEVENSON (b. 1933)

'The silver swan'

The silver swan, who living had no note,
When death approached unlocked her silent throat,
Leaning her breast against the reedy shore,
Thus sung her first and last, and sung no more:
Farewell all joys, O death come close mine eyes,
More geese than swans now live, more fools than wise.

ANON. (*c.* 1600)

The silver Swanne A setting by the court composer Orlando Gibbons of
this anonymous elegiac poem, in *The First Set of Madrigals and Mottets* (1612).
It has been suggested that the poem may refer to the death of Edmund
Spenser, in 1599. BL Royal Mus. 15.e.2 (10). By permission of The British
Library Board.

'So we'll go no more a-roving'

So we'll go no more a-roving
　　So late into the night,
Though the heart be still as loving,
　　And the moon be still as bright.

For the sword outwears its sheath,
　　And the soul wears out the breast,
And the heart must pause to breathe,
　　And Love itself have rest.

Though the night was made for loving,
　　And the day returns too soon,
Yet we'll go no more a-roving
　　By the light of the moon.

GEORGE GORDON, LORD BYRON (1788–1824)

Teeth

English Teeth, English Teeth!
Shining in the sun
A part of British heritage
Aye, each and every one.

English Teeth, Happy Teeth!
Always having fun
Clamping down on bits of fish
And sausages half done.

English Teeth! HEROES' Teeth!
Hear them click! and clack!
Let's sing a song of praise to them –
Three Cheers for the Brown Grey and Black.

SPIKE MILLIGAN (b. 1918)

Teeth   Drawing by the author, in *Silly Verse for Kids* © Spike Milligan,
by permission of Spike Milligan Productions.

To My First White Hairs

Hirsute hell chimney-spouts, black thunderthroes
confluence of coarse cloudfleeces – my head sir! – scourbrush
in bitumen, past fossil beyond fingers of light – until . . .!

Sudden sprung as corn stalk after rain, watered milk weak;
as lightning shrunk to ant's antenna, shrivelled
off the febrile sight of crickets in the sun –

THREE WHITE HAIRS! frail invaders of the undergrowth
interpret time. I view them, wired wisps, vibrant coiled
beneath a magnifying glass, milk-thread presages

Of the hoary phase. Weave then, weave o quickly weave
your sham veneration. Knit me webs of winter sagehood,
nightcap, and the fungoid sequins of a crown.

WOLE SOYINKA (b. 1935)

Riddle-Me-Ree

My first is in life (not contained within heart)
My second's in whole but never in part.
My third's in forever, but also in vain.
My last's in ending, why not in pain?

is love the answer?

LIZ LOCHHEAD (b. 1947)

The Expulsion from Eden

In either hand the hast'ning angel caught
Our ling'ring parents, and to th' eastern gate
Led them direct, and down the cliff as fast
To the subjected plain; then disappeared.
They looking back, all th' eastern side beheld
Of Paradise, so late their happy seat,
Waved over by that flaming brand, the gate
With dreadful faces thronged and fiery arms:
Some natural tears they dropped, but wiped them soon;
The world was all before them, where to choose
Their place of rest, and Providence their guide:
They hand in hand with wand'ring steps and slow,
Through Eden took their solitary way.

from PARADISE LOST, BOOK XII

JOHN MILTON (1608–74)

'There was an Old Man with a beard'

There was an Old Man with a beard,
Who said, "It is just as I feared! –
   Two Owls and a Hen,
   Four Larks and a Wren,
Have all built their nests in my beard!"
from THE BOOK OF NONSENSE

EDWARD LEAR (1812–88)

There was an Old Man with a beard   Drawing by the author, from
The Book of Nonsense

Spring and Fall
to a young child

Margaret, are you grieving
Over Goldengrove unleaving?
Leaves, like the things of man, you
With your fresh thoughts care for, can you?
Ah! as the heart grows older
It will come to such sights colder
By and by, nor spare a sigh
Though worlds of wanwood leafmeal lie;
And yet you *will* weep and know why.
Now no matter, child, the name:
Sorrow's springs are the same.
Nor mouth had, no nor mind, expressed
What heart heard of, ghost guessed:
It is the blight man was born for,
It is Margaret you mourn for.

GERARD MANLEY HOPKINS (1844–89)

Dog Days

'When you stop to consider
The days spent dreaming of a future
And say then, that was my life.'

For the days are long –
From the first milk van
To the last shout in the night,
An eternity. But the weeks go by
Like birds; and the years, the years
Fly past anti-clockwise
Like clock hands in a bar mirror.

DEREK MAHON (b. 1941)

The Visitor

In Spanish he whispers there is no time left.
It is the sound of scythes arcing in wheat,
the ache of some field song in Salvador.
The wind along the prison, cautious
as Francisco's hands on the inside, touching
the walls as he walks, it is his wife's breath
slipping into his cell each night while he
imagines his hand to be hers. It is a small country.

There is nothing one man will not do to another.

CAROLYN FORCHÉ (b. 1950)

Ariel's Song

Full fathom five thy father lies,
    Of his bones are coral made:
Those are pearls that were his eyes,
    Nothing of him that doth fade,
But doth suffer a sea-change
Into something rich, and strange:
Sea-nymphs hourly ring his knell –
    Hark! now I hear them,
      Ding-dong bell.

from THE TEMPEST

WILLIAM SHAKESPEARE (1564–1616)

Ariel   Illustration by Arthur Rackham

Meeting at Night

The grey sea and the long black land;
And the yellow half-moon large and low;
And the startled little waves that leap
In fiery ringlets from their sleep,
As I gain the cove with pushing prow,
And quench its speed i' the slushy sand.

Then a mile of warm sea-scented beach;
Three fields to cross till a farm appears;
A tap at the pane, the quick sharp scratch
And blue spurt of a lighted match,
And a voice less loud, thro' its joys and fears,
Than the two hearts beating each to each!

ROBERT BROWNING (1812–89)

Prelude I

The winter evening settles down
With smell of steaks in passageways.
Six o'clock.
The burnt-out ends of smoky days.
And now a gusty shower wraps
The grimy scraps
Of withered leaves about your feet
And newspapers from vacant lots;
The showers beat
On broken blinds and chimney-pots,
And at the corner of the street
A lonely cab-horse steams and stamps.

And then the lighting of the lamps.

T. S. ELIOT (1888–1965)

London Airport

Last night in London Airport
I saw a wooden bin
labelled UNWANTED LITERATURE
IS TO BE PLACED HEREIN.
So I wrote a poem
and popped it in.

CHRISTOPHER LOGUE (b. 1926)

Taid's Grave

Rain on lilac leaves. In the dusk
they show me the grave,
a casket of stars underfoot,
his name there, and his language.

Voice of thrushes in rain.
My cousin Gwynfor eases me
into the green cave.
Wet hands of lilac

touch my wrist and the secret
unfreckled underside of my arm
daring fingers to count
five warm blue eggs.

GILLIAN CLARKE (b. 1937)

Taid: Welsh for grandfather.

The Coming of Grendel

Now from the marshlands under the mist-mountains
Came Grendel prowling; branded with God's ire.
This murderous monster was minded to entrap
Some hapless human in that high hall.
On he came under the clouds, until clearly
He could see the great golden feasting place,
Glimmering wine-hall of men. Not his first
Raid was this on the homeplace of Hrothgar.
Never before though and never afterward
Did he encounter hardier defenders of a hall.

from BEOWULF (10th century or earlier)

translated by GERARD BENSON

In my Craft or Sullen Art

In my craft or sullen art
Exercised in the still night
When only the moon rages
And the lovers lie abed
With all their griefs in their arms,
I labour by singing light
Not for ambition or bread
Or the strut and trade of charms
On the ivory stages
But for the common wages
Of their most secret heart.

Not for the proud man apart
From the raging moon I write
On these spindrift pages
Nor for the towering dead
With their nightingales and psalms
But for the lovers, their arms
Round the griefs of the ages,
Who pay no praise or wages
Nor heed my craft or art.

DYLAN THOMAS (1914–53)

Midsummer, Tobago

Broad sun-stoned beaches.

White heat.
A green river.

A bridge,
scorched yellow palms

from the summer-sleeping house
drowsing through August.

Days I have held,
days I have lost,

days that outgrow, like daughters,
my harbouring arms.

DEREK WALCOTT (b. 1930)

How do I love thee? Autograph manuscript, with corrections, of one of the most popular 'Sonnets from the Portuguese'. BL Add. MS 43487, f.49. By permission of The British Library Board.

Sonnet from the Portuguese

How do I love thee? Let me count the ways.
I love thee to the depth and breadth and height
My soul can reach, when feeling out of sight
For the ends of Being and ideal Grace.
I love thee to the level of everyday's
Most quiet need, by sun and candlelight.
I love thee freely, as men strive for Right;
I love thee purely, as they turn from Praise.
I love thee with the passion put to use
In my old griefs, and with my childhood's faith.
I love thee with a love I seemed to lose
With my lost saints, – I love thee with the breath,
Smiles, tears, of all my life! – and, if God choose,
I shall but love thee better after death.

ELIZABETH BARRETT BROWNING (1806–61)

Handbag

My mother's old leather handbag,
crowded with letters she carried
all through the war. The smell
of my mother's handbag: mints
and lipstick and Coty powder.
The look of those letters, softened
and worn at the edges, opened,
read, and refolded so often.
Letters from my father. Odour
of leather and powder, which ever
since then has meant womanliness,
and love, and anguish, and war.

RUTH FAINLIGHT (b. 1931)

Symphony in Yellow

An omnibus across the bridge
   Crawls like a yellow butterfly,
   And, here and there, a passer-by
Shows like a little restless midge.

Big barges full of yellow hay
   Are moored against the shadowy wharf,
   And, like a yellow silken scarf,
The thick fog hangs along the quay.

The yellow leaves begin to fade
   And flutter from the Temple elms,
   And at my feet the pale green Thames
Lies like a rod of rippled jade.

OSCAR WILDE (1854–1900)

Caricature of Oscar Wilde
in a Top Hat. Black and white
drawing by Beatrice Whistler.
Birnie Philip Bequest. By
permission of The Hunterian
Art Gallery, University of
Glasgow.

'Sumer is icumen in'   English and Latin texts, with music, of the earliest known English round. The Latin text is completely unrelated to the English original. From a manuscript transcribed at Reading Abbey in the early thirteenth century. BL Harley 978. f.11v. By permission of The British Library Board.

'Sumer is icumen in'

Sumer is icumen in,
Loud sing cuckoo!
Groweth seed and bloweth mead
And springeth the wood now.
Sing cuckoo!

Ewe bleateth after lamb,
Cow loweth after calf,
Bullock starteth, buck farteth,
Merry sing cuckoo!

Cuckoo, cuckoo!
Well singest thou cuckoo,
Nor cease thou never now!

Sing cuckoo now, sing cuckoo!
Sing cuckoo, sing cuckoo now!

ANON. (13th century)

Song

Stop all the clocks, cut off the telephone,
Prevent the dog from barking with a juicy bone,
Silence the pianos and with muffled drum
Bring out the coffin, let the mourners come.

Let aeroplanes circle moaning overhead
Scribbling on the sky the message He Is Dead,
Put crêpe bows round the white necks of the public doves,
Let the traffic policemen wear black cotton gloves.

He was my North, my South, my East and West,
My working week and my Sunday rest,
My noon, my midnight, my talk, my song;
I thought that love would last for ever: I was wrong.

The stars are not wanted now; put out every one,
Pack up the moon and dismantle the sun,
Pour away the ocean and sweep up the wood;
For nothing now can ever come to any good.

W. H. AUDEN (1907–73)

The Ancients of the World

The salmon lying in the depths of Llyn Llifon,
  Secretly as a thought in a dark mind,
Is not so old as the owl of Cwm Cowlyd
  Who tells her sorrow nightly on the wind.

The ousel singing in the woods of Cilgwri,
  Tirelessly as a stream over the mossed stones,
Is not so old as the toad of Cors Fochno
  Who feels the cold skin sagging round his bones.

The toad and the ousel and the stag of Rhedynfre,
  That has cropped each leaf from the tree of life,
Are not so old as the owl of Cwm Cowlyd,
  That the proud eagle would have to wife.

R. S. THOMAS (b. 1913)

Day Trip

Two women, seventies, hold hands
on the edge of Essex,
hair in strong nets,
shrieked laughter echoing gulls
as shingle sucks from under feet
easing in brine.

There must be an unspoken point
when the sea feels like
their future. No longer paddling,
ankles submerge in lace,
in satin ripple.
Dress hems darken.

They do not risk their balance
for the shimmering of ships
at the horizon's sweep
as, thigh deep, they inch on
fingers splayed, wrists bent,
learning to walk again.

CAROLE SATYAMURTI (b. 1939)

In Time of 'The Breaking of Nations'

I

Only a man harrowing clods
  In a slow silent walk
With an old horse that stumbles and nods
  Half asleep as they stalk.

II

Only thin smoke without flame
  From the heaps of couch-grass;
Yet this will go onward the same
  Though Dynasties pass.

III

Yonder a maid and her wight
  Come whispering by:
War's annals will cloud into night
  Ere their story die.

THOMAS HARDY (1840–1928)

'Thou art my battle axe and weapons of war: for with thee will I break in pieces the nations, and with thee will I destroy kingdoms' (Jeremiah: 51.20).

London Bells

Two sticks and an apple,
Ring the bells at Whitechapel.

Old Father Bald Pate,
Ring the bells Aldgate.

Maids in white aprons,
Ring the bells at St. Catherine's.

Oranges and lemons,
Ring the bells at St. Clement's.

When will you pay me?
Ring the bells at the Old Bailey.

When I am rich,
Ring the bells at Fleetditch.

When will that be?
Ring the bells at Stepney.

When I am old,
Ring the great bell at Paul's.

ANON. (early 18th century)

London Bells.

Two Sticks & an Apple,
Ring ỹ Bells at Whitechapple
Old Father Bald Pate,
Ring ỹ Bells Aldgate,
Maids in white Aprons,
Ring ỹ Bells ɔ S.ᵗCathrines,

Oranges

Oranges and Lemmons,
Ring ỹ Bells at S.ᵗClemens,
When will you pay me,
Ring ỹ Bells at ỹ Old Bailey,
When I am Rich,
Ring ỹ Bells at Fleet ditch,
When will that be,
Ring ỹ Bells at Stepney,
When I am Old,
Ring ỹ great Bell at Pauls.

London Bells   The traditional London rhyme as it appears in an early hand-set printed children's book, *Tommy Thumb's Pretty Song Book* (1744), Vol. II. By permission of The British Library Board.

The Tyger A much-corrected autograph draft of the poem, in Blake's notebook, the 'Rossetti Manuscript'. BL Add. MS 49460, f.56. By permission of The British Library Board.

The Tyger

Tyger Tyger, burning bright,
In the forests of the night;
What immortal hand or eye,
Could frame thy fearful symmetry?

In what distant deeps or skies
Burnt the fire of thine eyes!
On what wings dare he aspire?
What the hand, dare sieze the fire?

And what shoulder, & what art,
Could twist the sinews of thy heart?
And when thy heart began to beat,
What dread hand? & what dread feet?

What the hammer? what the chain?
In what furnace was thy brain?
What the anvil? what dread grasp,
Dare its deadly terrors clasp?

When the stars threw down their spears
And water'd heaven with their tears:
Did he smile his work to see?
Did he who made the Lamb make thee?

Tyger Tyger, burning bright,
In the forests of the night:
What immortal hand or eye,
Dare frame thy fearful symmetry?

WILLIAM BLAKE (1757–1827)

Delay

The radiance of that star that leans on me
Was shining years ago. The light that now
Glitters up there my eye may never see,
And so the time lag teases me with how

Love that loves now may not reach me until
Its first desire is spent. The star's impulse
Must wait for eyes to claim it beautiful
And love arrived may find us somewhere else.

ELIZABETH JENNINGS (b. 1926)

Everything Changes
after Brecht, *'Alles wandelt sich'*

Everything changes. We plant
trees for those born later
but what's happened has happened,
and poisons poured into the seas
cannot be drained out again.

What's happened has happened.
Poisons poured into the seas
cannot be drained out again, but
everything changes. We plant
trees for those born later.

CICELY HERBERT (b. 1937)

Roundel

Now welcome Summer with thy sunnė soft,
That hast this winter's weathers overshake,
And driven away the longė nightės black.

Saint Valentine, that art full high aloft,
Thus singen smallė fowlės for thy sake:
Now welcome Summer with thy sunnė soft,
That hast this winter's weathers overshake.

Well have they cause for to gladden oft,
Since each of them recovered hath his make.
Full blissful may they singė when they wake:
Now welcome Summer with thy sunnė soft,
That hast this winter's weathers overshake,
And driven away the longė nightės black!

from THE PARLIAMENT OF FOWLS

GEOFFREY CHAUCER (1340?–1400)

Introduction to *The Parliament of Fowls* from a fifteenth-century copy of
Chaucer's Works in the Cambridge University Library. GG.4.27, f.480b. By
permission of the Syndics of Cambridge University Library.

Dreams

Here we are all, by day; by night we're hurled
By dreams, each one, into a several world.

ROBERT HERRICK (1591–1674)

Sonnet

What lips my lips have kissed, and where, and why,
I have forgotten, and what arms have lain
Under my head till morning; but the rain
Is full of ghosts tonight, that tap and sigh
Upon the glass and listen for reply,
And in my heart there stirs a quiet pain
For unremembered lads that not again
Will turn to me at midnight with a cry.
Thus in the winter stands the lonely tree,
Nor knows what birds have vanished one by one,
Yet knows its boughs more silent than before:
I cannot say what loves have come and gone,
I only know that summer sang in me
A little while, that in me sings no more.

EDNA ST. VINCENT MILLAY (1892–1950)

And Yet the Books

And yet the books will be there on the shelves, separate beings,
That appeared once, still wet
As shining chestnuts under a tree in autumn,
And, touched, coddled, began to live
In spite of fires on the horizon, castles blown up,
Tribes on the march, planets in motion.
"We are," they said, even as their pages
Were being torn out, or a buzzing flame
Licked away their letters. So much more durable
Than we are, whose frail warmth
Cools down with memory, disperses, perishes.
I imagine the earth when I am no more:
Nothing happens, no loss, it's still a strange pageant,
Women's dresses, dewy lilacs, a song in the valley.
Yet the books will be there on the shelves, well born,
Derived from people, but also from radiance, heights.

CZESLAW MILOSZ (b. 1911)
translated by CZESLAW MILOSZ AND ROBERT HASS

The Leader

I wanna be the leader
I wanna be the leader
Can I be the leader?
Can I? I can?
Promise? Promise?
Yippee, I'm the leader
I'm the leader

OK what shall we do?

ROGER McGOUGH (b. 1937)

from **To the City of London**

Above all rivers thy river hath renown,
Whose beryl streamẻs, pleasant and preclare,
Under thy lusty wallẻs runneth down;
Where many a swan doth swim with wingẻs fair,
Where many a barge doth sail, and row with oar,
Where many a ship doth rest with top-royal.
O town of townẻs, patron and not compare,
London, thou art the flower of Cities all.

WILLIAM DUNBAR (1465?–1530?)

To the City of London   The 'river' stanza. The full text of the poem is
copied into *The Chronicle of London 1215–1509*, where the poem is said to have
been 'made' while the company was sitting at dinner. BL Cotton MS Vitell.
A.XVI, f.200v. By permission of The British Library Board.

On First Looking into Chapman's Homer

Much have I travell'd in the realms of gold,
   And many goodly states and kingdoms seen;
   Round many western islands have I been
Which bards in fealty to Apollo hold.
Oft of one wide expanse had I been told
   That deep-brow'd Homer ruled as his demesne;
   Yet did I never breathe its pure serene
Till I heard Chapman speak out loud and bold:
Then felt I like some watcher of the skies
   When a new planet swims into his ken;
Or like stout Cortez when with eagle eyes
   He star'd at the Pacific – and all his men
Look'd at each other with a wild surmise –
   Silent, upon a peak in Darien.

JOHN KEATS (1795–1821)

A Dead Statesman

I could not dig: I dared not rob:
Therefore I lied to please the mob.
Now all my lies are proved untrue
And I must face the men I slew.
What tale shall serve me here among
Mine angry and defrauded young?

from EPITAPHS OF THE WAR 1914–18

RUDYARD KIPLING (1865–1936)

Modern Secrets

Last night I dreamt in Chinese.
Eating Yankee shredded wheat
I said it in English
To a friend who answered
In monosyllables:
All of which I understood.

The dream shrank to its fiction.
I had understood its end
Many years ago. The sallow child
Ate rice from its ricebowl
And hides still in the cupboard
With the china and tea-leaves.

SHIRLEY GEOK-LIN LIM (b. 1944)

Sergeant Brown's Parrot

Many policemen wear upon their shoulders
Cunning little radios. To pass away the time
They talk about the traffic to them, listen to the news,
And it helps them to Keep Down Crime.

But Sergeant Brown, he wears upon his shoulder
A tall green parrot as he's walking up and down
And all the parrot says is "Who's-a-pretty-boy-then?"
"I am," says Sergeant Brown.

KIT WRIGHT (b. 1944)

Sergeant Brown's Parrot   Drawing by Posy Simmonds, © Posy
Simmonds. By permission of Collins Publishers.

'I have a gentil cock'

I have a gentil cock, croweth me day
he doth me risen early, my matins for to say

I have a gentil cock, comen he is of great
his comb is of red coral, his tail is of jet

I have a gentil cock, comen he is of kind
his comb is of red sorrel, his tail is of inde

his legs be of azure, so gentil and so small
his spurs are of silver white, into the wortewale

his eyes are of crystal, locked all in amber
and every night he percheth him in my lady's chamber

ANON. (early 15th century)

'I have a gentil cook [cock]'   From a collection dating from the early
15th century, and attributed to the monastery of Bury St Edmunds, containing
the only surviving copies of over 70 early English carols and other lyrics.
BL MS Sloane 2593, f.10b. By permission of The British Library Board.

What Am I After All

What am I after all but a child, pleas'd with the sound of
    my own name? repeating it over and over;
I stand apart to hear – it never tires me.

To you your name also;
Did you think there was nothing but two or three
    pronunciations in the sound of your name?

WALT WHITMAN (1819–92)

Piano

Softly, in the dusk, a woman is singing to me;
Taking me back down the vista of years, till I see
A child sitting under the piano, in the boom of the tingling
    strings
And pressing the small, poised feet of a mother who smiles as
    she sings.

In spite of myself, the insidious mastery of song
Betrays me back, till the heart of me weeps to belong
To the old Sunday evenings at home, with winter outside
And hymns in the cosy parlour, the tinkling piano our guide.

So now it is vain for the singer to burst into clamour
With the great black piano appassionato. The glamour
Of childish days is upon me, my manhood is cast
Down in the flood of remembrance, I weep like a child for the
    past.

D. H. LAWRENCE (1885–1930)

Mmenson

Summon now the kings of the forest,
horn of the elephant,
mournful call of the elephant;

summon the emirs, kings of the desert,
horses caparisoned, beaten gold bent,
archers and criers, porcupine arrows, bows bent;

recount now the gains and the losses:
Agades, Sokoto, El Hassan dead in his tent,
the silks and the brasses, the slow weary tent

of our journeys down slopes, dry river courses;
land of the lion, land of the leopard, elephant
country; tall grasses, thick prickly herbs. Blow elephant

trumpet; summon the horses,
dead horses, our losses: the bent
slow bow of the Congo, the watering Niger . . .

EDWARD KAMAU BRATHWAITE (b. 1930)

Light

I live for books
and light to read them in.
                          Waterlilies
reaching up
from the depths of the pond
algae dark,
the frog loves a jell of
blue-green water,
                          the bud
scales
a rope of stem,
then floats in sunshine. Like soap
in the morning bath.
This book I read
floats in my hand like a waterlily
coming out of the nutrient waters
of thought
and light shines on us both,
the morning's breviary.

DIANE WAKOSKI (b. 1937)

from The Song of Solomon

My beloved spake, and said unto me, Rise up, my love, my fair
    one, and come away.
For lo, the winter is past, the rain is over, and gone.
The flowers appear on the earth, the time of the singing of
    birds is come, and the voice of the turtle is heard in our
    land.
The fig tree putteth forth her green figs, and the vines with
    the tender grape give a good smell.
Arise, my love, my fair one, and come away.

THE KING JAMES BIBLE (1611)

'You took away all the oceans and all the room'

You took away all the oceans and all the room.
You gave me my shoe-size in earth with bars around it.
Where did it get you? Nowhere.
You left me my lips, and they shape words, even in silence.

OSIP MANDELSTAM (1891–1938)
translated by CLARENCE BROWN AND W. S. MERWIN

Wet Evening in April

The birds sang in the wet trees
And as I listened to them it was a hundred years from now
And I was dead and someone else was listening to them.
But I was glad I had recorded for him
  The melancholy.

PATRICK KAVANAGH (1906–67)

I Saw a Jolly Hunter

I saw a jolly hunter
   With a jolly gun
Walking in the country
   In the jolly sun.

   In the jolly meadow
     Sat a jolly hare.
   Saw the jolly hunter.
     Took jolly care.

Hunter jolly eager –
   Sight of jolly prey.
Forgot gun pointing
   Wrong jolly way.

   Jolly hunter jolly head
     Over heels gone.
   Jolly old safety catch
     Not jolly on.

     Bang went the jolly gun.
       Hunter jolly dead.
     Jolly hare got clean away.
       Jolly good, I said.

CHARLES CAUSLEY (b. 1917)

I Saw a Jolly Hunter Drawing by
Pat Marriott, from *Figgie Hobbin*.
By permission of Macmillan London.

Aunt Jennifer's Tigers

Aunt Jennifer's tigers prance across a screen,
Bright topaz denizens of a world of green.
They do not fear the men beneath the tree;
They pace in sleek chivalric certainty.

Aunt Jennifer's fingers fluttering through her wool
Find even the ivory needle hard to pull.
The massive weight of Uncle's wedding band
Sits heavily upon Aunt Jennifer's hand.

When Aunt is dead, her terrified hands will lie
Still ringed with ordeals she was mastered by.
The tigers in the panel that she made
Will go on prancing, proud and unafraid.

ADRIENNE RICH (b. 1929)

Old English Riddle

A moth, I thought, munching a word.
How marvellously weird! a worm
Digesting a man's sayings –
A sneakthief nibbling in the shadows
At the shape of a poet's thunderous phrases –
How unutterably strange!
And the pilfering parasite none the wiser
For the words he has swallowed.

from THE EXETER BOOK
translated by GERARD BENSON

Answer: Bookworm

Old English Riddle from *The Exeter Book*, a manuscript of about the year 1000,
containing over ninety riddles and several other Old English poems. Reprinted
with the permission of the Dean and Chapter of Exeter Cathedral.

Virtue

Sweet day, so cool, so calm, so bright,
The bridal of the earth and sky:
The dew shall weep thy fall tonight;
                        For thou must die.

Sweet rose, whose hue angry and brave
Bids the rash gazer wipe his eye:
Thy root is ever in its grave,
                        And thou must die.

Sweet spring, full of sweet days and roses,
A box where sweets compacted lie;
My music shows ye have your closes,
                        And all must die.

Only a sweet and virtuous soul,
Like seasoned timber, never gives;
But though the whole world turn to coal,
                        Then chiefly lives.

GEORGE HERBERT (1593–1633)

'I know the truth – give up all other truths!'

I know the truth – give up all other truths!
No need for people anywhere on earth to struggle.
Look – it is evening, look, it is nearly night:
what do you speak of, poets, lovers, generals?

The wind is level now, the earth is wet with dew,
the storm of stars in the sky will turn to quiet.
And soon all of us will sleep under the earth, we
who never let each other sleep above it.

1915

MARINA TSVETAYEVA (1892–1941)
translated by ELAINE FEINSTEIN

Love Without Hope

Love without hope, as when the young bird-catcher
Swept off his tall hat to the Squire's own daughter,
So let the imprisoned larks escape and fly
Singing about her head, as she rode by.

ROBERT GRAVES (1895–1985)

Full Moon and Little Frieda

A cool small evening shrunk to a dog bark and the clank
                                   of a bucket –

And you listening.
A spider's web, tense for the dew's touch.
A pail lifted, still and brimming – mirror
To tempt a first star to a tremor.

Cows are going home in the lane there, looping the hedges
                         with their warm wreaths of breath –
A dark river of blood, many boulders,
Balancing unspilled milk.

'Moon!' you cry suddenly, 'Moon! Moon!'

The moon has stepped back like an artist gazing amazed
                                   at a work
That points at him amazed.

TED HUGHES (b. 1930)

'Since there's no help, come let us kiss and part'

Since there's no help, come let us kiss and part,
Nay, I have done: you get no more of me,
And I am glad, yea glad with all my heart
That thus so cleanly I myself can free,
Shake hands forever, cancel all our vows,
And when we meet at any time again,
Be it not seen in either of our brows
That we one jot of former love retain.
Now at the last gasp of love's latest breath,
When his pulse failing, passion speechless lies,
When faith is kneeling by his bed of death,
And innocence is closing up his eyes,
   Now if thou wouldst, when all have given him over,
   From death to life thou mightst him yet recover.

MICHAEL DRAYTON (1563–1631)

'Into my heart an air that kills'

Into my heart an air that kills
   From yon far country blows:
What are those blue remembered hills,
   What spires, what farms are those?

That is the land of lost content,
   I see it shining plain,
The happy highways where I went
   And cannot come again.

from A SHROPSHIRE LAD

A. E. HOUSMAN (1859–1936)

Dolor

I have known the inexorable sadness of pencils,
Neat in their boxes, dolor of pad and paper-weight,
All the misery of manilla folders and mucilage,
Desolation in immaculate public places,
Lonely reception room, lavatory, switchboard,
The unalterable pathos of basin and pitcher,
Ritual of multigraph, paper-clip, comma,
Endless duplication of lives and objects.
And I have seen dust from the walls of institutions,
Finer than flour, alive, more dangerous than silica,
Sift, almost invisible, through long afternoons of tedium,
Dropping a fine film on nails and delicate eyebrows,
Glazing the pale hair, the duplicate grey standard faces.

THEODORE ROETHKE (1908–63)

The Cries of London

Here's fine rosemary, sage, and thyme.
Come buy my ground ivy.
Here's fetherfew, gilliflowers and rue.
Come buy my knotted marjorum, ho!
Come buy my mint, my fine green mint.
Here's fine lavender for your cloaths.
Here's parsley and winter-savory,
And hearts-ease, which all do choose.
Here's balm and hissop, and cinquefoil,
All fine herbs, it is well known.
    Let none despise the merry, merry cries
    Of famous London-town!

Here's fine herrings, eight a groat.
Hot codlins, pies and tarts.
New mackerel! have to sell.
Come buy my Wellfleet oysters, ho!
Come buy my whitings fine and new.
Wives, shall I mend your husbands horns?
I'll grind your knives to please your wives,
And very nicely cut your corns.
Maids, have you any hair to sell,
Either flaxen, black, or brown?
    Let none despise the merry, merry cries
    Of famous London-town!

ANON. (17th century)

The Cries of London   A setting by Orlando Gibbons of several London 'Cries' for five singers and five viol players. BL. Add.MS 29373, f.33v. By permission of The British Library Board.

A 5.

Good sausage

New oysters new, new plaiſe new   new

mackerell new,

Ha' ye any kitchmstuffe mayds.

Ha ye any kitchmstuffe mayds

I ha' ripe cowcumbers ripe

Salt, salt, salt to barge to, Hard onyons hard, AΓ a black

A 14-Year-Old Convalescent Cat in the Winter

I want him to have another living summer,
to lie in the sun and enjoy the *douceur de vivre* –
because the sun, like golden rum in a rummer,
is what makes an idle cat *un tout petit peu ivre* –

I want him to lie stretched out, contented,
revelling in the heat, his fur all dry and warm,
an Old Age Pensioner, retired, resented
by no one, and happinesses in a beelike swarm

to settle on him – postponed for another season
that last fated hateful journey to the vet
from which there is no return (and age the reason),
which must soon come – as I cannot forget.

GAVIN EWART (b. 1916)

Come. And Be My Baby

The highway is full of big cars
going nowhere fast
And folks is smoking anything that'll burn
Some people wrap their lives around a cocktail glass
And you sit wondering
where you're going to turn.
I got it.
Come. And be my baby.

Some prophets say the world is gonna end tomorrow
But others say we've got a week or two
The paper is full of every kind of blooming horror
And you sit wondering
what you're gonna do.
I got it.
Come. And be my baby.

MAYA ANGELOU (b. 1928)

'Ich am of Irlonde'

I am of Ireland,
And of the holy land
Of Ireland.

Good sir, pray I thee,
For of saint charity,
Come and dance with me
In Ireland.

ANON. (14th century)

Song

Now sleeps the crimson petal, now the white;
Nor waves the cypress in the palace walk;
Nor winks the gold fin in the porphyry font:
The fire-fly wakens: waken thou with me.

Now droops the milkwhite peacock like a ghost,
And like a ghost she glimmers on to me.

Now lies the Earth all Danaë to the stars,
And all thy heart lies open unto me.

Now slides the silent meteor on, and leaves
A shining furrow, as thy thoughts in me.

Now folds the lily all her sweetness up,
And slips into the bosom of the lake:
So fold thyself, my dearest, thou, and slip
Into my bosom and be lost in me.

from THE PRINCESS

ALFRED, LORD TENNYSON (1809–92)

The Embankment

(The Fantasia of a Fallen Gentleman on a Cold, Bitter Night)

Once, in finesse of fiddles found I ecstasy,
In a flash of gold heels on the hard pavement.
Now see I
That warmth's the very stuff of poesy.
Oh, God, make small
The old star-eaten blanket of the sky,
That I may fold it round me and in comfort lie.

T. E. HULME (1883–1917)

Stars and planets

Trees are cages for them: water holds its breath
To balance them without smudging on its delicate meniscus.
Children watch them playing in their heavenly playground;
Men use them to lug ships across oceans, through firths.

They seem so twinkle-still, but they never cease
Inventing new spaces and huge explosions
And migrating in mathematical tribes over
The steppes of space at their outrageous ease.

It's hard to think that the earth is one –
This poor sad bearer of wars and disasters
Rolls-Roycing round the sun with its load of gangsters,
Attended only by the loveless moon.

NORMAN MacCAIG (b. 1910)

The Uncertainty of the Poet

I am a poet.
I am very fond of bananas.

I am bananas.
I am very fond of a poet.

I am a poet of bananas.
I am very fond.

A fond poet of 'I am, I am' –
Very bananas.

Fond of 'Am I bananas?
Am I?' – a very poet.

Bananas of a poet!
Am I fond? Am I very?

Poet bananas! I am.
I am fond of a 'very'.

I am of very fond bananas.
Am I a poet?

WENDY COPE (b. 1945)

'I saw a Peacock with a fiery tail'

I saw a Peacock with a fiery tail
I saw a blazing Comet drop down hail
I saw a Cloud with Ivy circled round
I saw a sturdy Oak creep on the ground
I saw a Pismire swallow up a Whale
I saw a raging Sea brim full of Ale
I saw a Venice Glass sixteen foot deep
I saw a Well full of men's tears that weep
I saw their Eyes all in a flame of fire
I saw a House as big as the Moon and higher
I saw the Sun even in the midst of night
I saw the Man that saw this wondrous sight.

ANON. (17th century)

from **Frost at Midnight**

The Frost performs its secret ministry,
Unhelped by any wind. The owlet's cry
Came loud – and hark, again! loud as before.
The inmates of my cottage, all at rest,
Have left me to that solitude, which suits
Abstruser musings: save that at my side
My cradled infant slumbers peacefully.
'Tis calm indeed! so calm, that it disturbs
And vexes meditation with its strange
And extreme silentness. Sea, hill, and wood,
This populous village! Sea, and hill, and wood,
With all the numberless goings-on of life,
Inaudible as dreams!

SAMUEL TAYLOR COLERIDGE (1772–1834)

Snow

The room was suddenly rich and the great bay-window was
Spawning snow and pink roses against it
Soundlessly collateral and incompatible:
World is suddener than we fancy it.

World is crazier and more of it than we think,
Incorrigibly plural. I peel and portion
A tangerine and spit the pips and feel
The drunkenness of things being various.

And the fire flames with a bubbling sound for world
Is more spiteful and gay than one supposes –
On the tongue on the eyes on the ears in the palms of one's
     hands –
There is more than glass between the snow and the huge
     roses.

LOUIS MacNEICE (1907–63)

On Himself

Abstracted by silence from the age of seven,
Deafened and penned by as black calamity
As twice to be born, I cannot without pity
Contemplate myself as an infant;

Or fail to speak of silence as a priestess
Calling to serve in the temple of a skull
Her innocent choice. It is barely possible
Not to be affected by such a distress.

DAVID WRIGHT (b. 1920)

Sometimes

Sometimes things don't go, after all,
from bad to worse. Some years, muscadel
faces down frost; green thrives; the crops don't fail,
sometimes a man aims high, and all goes well.

A people sometimes will step back from war;
elect an honest man; decide they care
enough, that they can't leave some stranger poor.
Some men become what they were born for.

Sometimes our best efforts do not go
amiss; sometimes we do as we meant to.
The sun will sometimes melt a field of sorrow
that seemed hard frozen: may it happen for you.

SHEENAGH PUGH (b. 1950)

The Passionate Shepherd to his Love

Come live with me, and be my love,
And we will all the pleasures prove
That valleys, groves, hills and fields,
Woods, or steepy mountain yields.

And we will sit upon the rocks,
Seeing the shepherds feed their flocks
By shallow rivers, to whose falls
Melodious birds sing madrigals.

And I will make thee beds of roses,
And a thousand fragrant posies,
A cap of flowers, and a kirtle,
Embroidered all with leaves of myrtle.

A gown made of the finest wool
Which from our pretty lambs we pull,
Fair lined slippers for the cold,
With buckles of the purest gold.

A belt of straw and ivy buds,
With coral clasps and amber studs,
And if these pleasures may thee move,
Come live with me, and be my love.

The shepherds' swains shall dance and sing
For thy delight each May-morning;
If these delights thy mind may move,
Then live with me, and be my love.

CHRISTOPHER MARLOWE (1564–93)

Letter to André Billy. 9 April 1915

Gunner/Driver One (front-line)
Here I am and send you greetings
No no you're not seeing things
My Sector's number fifty-nine

I hear the whistle of
the   the bird
beautiful bird of p^re^y

I see^{far away}   O   D
the cathed^{ral}   H   E
                          M   A
                          Y   A R
                          N D R E
                          B I L L Y

GUILLAUME APOLLINAIRE (1880–1918)

translated by OLIVER BERNARD

Child

Your clear eye is the one absolutely beautiful thing.
I want to fill it with colour and ducks,
The zoo of the new

Whose names you meditate –
April snowdrop, Indian pipe,
Little

Stalk without wrinkle,
Pool in which images
Should be grand and classical

Not this troublous
Wringing of hands, this dark
Ceiling without a star.

SYLVIA PLATH (1932–63)

A song for England

An' a so de rain a-fall
An' a so de snow a-rain

An' a so de fog a-fall
An' a so de sun a-fail

An' a so de seasons mix
An' a so de bag-o'-tricks

But a so me understan'
De misery o' de Englishman.

ANDREW SALKEY (b. 1928)

Letters from Yorkshire

In February, digging his garden, planting potatoes,
he saw the first lapwings return and came
indoors to write to me, his knuckles singing

as they reddened in the warmth.
It's not romance, simply how things are.
You out there, in the cold, seeing the seasons

turning, me with my heartful of headlines
feeding words onto a blank screen.
Is your life more real because you dig and sow?

You wouldn't say so, breaking ice on a waterbutt,
clearing a path through snow. Still, it's you
who sends me word of that other world

pouring air and light into an envelope. So that
at night, watching the same news in different houses,
our souls tap out messages across the icy miles.

MAURA DOOLEY (b. 1957)

136

The Bonnie Broukit Bairn

Mars is braw in crammasy,
Venus in a green silk goun,
The auld mune shak's her gowden feathers,
Their starry talk's a wheen o' blethers,
Nane for thee a thochtie sparin',
Earth, thou bonnie broukit bairn!
– *But greet, an' in your tears ye'll drown*
The haill clanjamfrie!

HUGH MacDIARMID (CHRISTOPHER MURRAY GRIEVE)
(1892–1978)

braw: fine
crammasy: crimson
a wheen o' blethers: a pack of nonsense
broukit: neglected
greet: weep
the haill clanjamfrie: the whole caboodle

To Emilia V –

Music, when soft voices die,
Vibrates in the memory –
Odours, when sweet violets sicken,
Live within the sense they quicken.

Rose leaves, when the rose is dead,
Are heaped for the beloved's bed –
And so thy thoughts, when thou art gone,
Love itself shall slumber on . . .

PERCY BYSSHE SHELLEY (1792–1822)

Concerto for Double Bass

He is a drunk leaning companionably
Around a lamp post or doing up
With intermittent concentration
Another drunk's coat.

He is a polite but devoted Valentino,
Cheek to cheek, forgetting the next step.
He is feeling the pulse of the fat lady
Or cutting her in half.

But close your eyes and it is sunset
At the edge of the world. It is the language
Of dolphins, the growth of tree-roots,
The heart-beat slowing down.

JOHN FULLER (b. 1937)

Words, Wide Night

Somewhere on the other side of this wide night
and the distance between us, I am thinking of you.
The room is turning slowly away from the moon.

This is pleasurable. Or shall I cross that out and say
it is sad? In one of the tenses I singing
an impossible song of desire that you cannot hear.

La lala la. See? I close my eyes and imagine
the dark hills I would have to cross
to reach you. For I am in love with you and this

is what it is like or what it is like in words.

CAROL ANN DUFFY (b. 1955)

The Lobster Quadrille

'Will you walk a little faster?' said a whiting to a snail,
'There's a porpoise close behind us, and he's treading on my tail.
See how eagerly the lobsters and the turtles all advance!
They are waiting on the shingle – will you come and join the dance?
  Will you, won't you, will you, won't you, will you join the dance?
  Will you, won't you, will you, won't you, won't you join the dance?

'You can really have no notion how delightful it will be
When they take us up and throw us, with the lobsters, out to sea!'
But the snail replied 'Too far, too far!', and gave a look askance –
Said he thanked the whiting kindly, but he would not join the dance.
  Would not, could not, would not, could not, would not join the dance.
  Would not, could not, would not, could not, could not join the dance.

'What matters it how far we go?' his scaly friend replied.
'There is another shore, you know, upon the other side.
The further off from England the nearer is to France –
Then turn not pale, beloved snail, but come and join the dance.
  Will you, won't you, will you, won't you, will you join the dance?
  Will you, won't you, will you, won't you, won't you join the dance?'

LEWIS CARROLL (1832–98)

———

The Lobster Quadrille   Illustration by John Tenniel.

'I shall say what inordinate love is'

I shall say what inordinate love is:
The furiosity and wodness of mind,
An instinguible burning, faulting bliss,
A great hunger, insatiate to find,
A dulcet ill, an evil sweetness blind,
A right wonderful sugared sweet error,
Without labour rest, contrary to kind,
Or without quiet, to have huge labour.

ANON. (15th century)

wodness: frenzy

Inordinate love The only known source of this English version of a well-known Latin original. Thott 110, 4to., f. 163a. By permission of The Copenhagen Royal Library.

A red red Rose

O my Luve 's like a red, red rose,
   That's newly sprung in June;
O my Luve 's like the melodie
   That's sweetly play'd in tune.

As fair art thou, my bonnie lass,
   So deep in luve am I;
And I will love thee still, my Dear,
   Till a' the seas gang dry.

Till a' the seas gang dry, my Dear,
   And the rocks melt wi' the sun:
I will love thee still, my Dear,
   While the sands o' life shall run.

And fare thee weel, my only Luve!
   And fare thee weel, a while!
And I will come again, my Luve,
   Tho' it were ten thousand mile!

ROBERT BURNS (1759–96)

The Very Leaves of the Acacia-Tree are London

The very leaves of the acacia-tree are London;
London tap-water fills out the fuschia buds in the back garden,
Blackbirds pull London worms out of the sour soil,
The woodlice, centipedes, eat London, the wasps even.
London air through stomata of myriad leaves
And million lungs of London breathes.
Chlorophyll and haemoglobin do what life can
To purify, to return this great explosion
To sanity of leaf and wing.
Gradual and gentle the growth of London Pride,
And sparrows are free of all the time in the world:
Less than a window-pane between.

KATHLEEN RAINE (b. 1908)

One Art

The art of losing isn't hard to master;
so many things seem filled with the intent
to be lost that their loss is no disaster.

Lose something every day. Accept the fluster
of lost door keys, the hour badly spent.
The art of losing isn't hard to master.

Then practice losing farther, losing faster:
places, and names, and where it was you meant
to travel. None of these will bring disaster.

I lost my mother's watch. And look! my last, or
next-to-last, of three loved houses went.
The art of losing isn't hard to master.

I lost two cities, lovely ones. And, vaster,
some realms I owned, two rivers, a continent.
I miss them, but it wasn't a disaster.

– Even losing you (the joking voice, a gesture
I love) I shan't have lied. It's evident
the art of losing's not too hard to master
though it may look like (*Write* it!) like disaster.

ELIZABETH BISHOP (1911–79)

To Someone Who Insisted I Look Up Someone

I rang them up while touring Timbuctoo,
Those bosom chums to whom you're known as *'Who?'*

X. J. KENNEDY (b. 1929)

Two Fragments

As a gale on the mountainside bends the oak tree
I am rocked by my love

Love holds me captive again
and I tremble with bittersweet longing

SAPPHO (fl. 600 BC)

translated by CICELY HERBERT

I Am

I am – yet what I am none cares or knows,
My friends forsake me like a memory lost;
I am the self-consumer of my woes,
They rise and vanish in oblivious host
Like shades in love and death's oblivion lost,
And yet I am – and live, with shadows tossed

Into the nothingness of scorn and noise,
Into the living sea of waking dreams,
Where there is neither sense of life nor joys,
But the vast shipwreck of my life's esteems;
And e'en the dearest, that I loved the best,
Are strange – nay, rather stranger than the rest.

I long for scenes where man has never trod,
A place where woman never smiled or wept,
There to abide with my creator, God,
And sleep as I in childhood sweetly slept,
Untroubling and untroubled where I lie;
The grass below – above the vaulted sky.

JOHN CLARE (1793–1864)

Dream Boogie

Good morning, daddy!
Ain't you heard
The boogie-woogie rumble
Of a dream deferred?

Listen closely:
You'll hear their feet
Beating out and beating out a –

> *You think*
> *It's a happy beat?*

Listen to it closely:
Ain't you heard
something underneath
like a –

> *What did I say?*

Sure,
I'm happy!
Take it away!

> *Hey, pop!*
> *Re-bop!*
> *Mop!*

> *Y–e–a–h!*

LANGSTON HUGHES (1902–67)

The Unpredicted

The goddess Fortune be praised (on her toothed wheel
I have been mincemeat these several years)
Last night, for a whole night, the unpredictable
Lay in my arms, in a tender and unquiet rest –
(I perceived the irrelevance of my former tears) –
Lay, and at dawn departed. I rose and walked the streets
Where a whitsuntide wind blew fresh, and blackbirds
Incontestably sang, and the people were beautiful.

JOHN HEATH-STUBBS (b. 1918)

The Emigrant Irish

Like oil lamps we put them out the back,

of our houses, of our minds. We had lights
better than, newer than and then

a time came, this time and now
we need them. Their dread, makeshift example.

They would have thrived on our necessities.
What they survived we could not even live.
By their lights now it is time to
imagine how they stood there, what they stood with,
that their possessions may become our power.

Cardboard. Iron. Their hardships parcelled in them.
Patience. Fortitude. Long-suffering
in the bruise-coloured dusk of the New World.

And all the old songs. And nothing to lose.

EAVAN BOLAND (b. 1944)

from **The Garden**

What wondrous life in this I lead!
Ripe apples drop about my head;
The luscious clusters of the vine
Upon my mouth do crush their wine;
The nectarine, and curious peach,
Into my hands themselves do reach;
Stumbling on melons, as I pass,
Ensnared with flowers, I fall on grass.

Meanwhile the mind, from pleasure less,
Withdraws into its happiness:
The mind, that ocean where each kind
Does straight its own resemblance find;
Yet it creates, transcending these,
Far other worlds, and other seas;
Annihilating all that's made
To a green thought in a green shade.

ANDREW MARVELL (1621–78)

The Flaw in Paganism

Drink and dance and laugh and lie,
    Love, the reeling midnight through,
For tomorrow we shall die!
    (But, alas, we never do.)

DOROTHY PARKER (1893–1967)

The Algonquin Round Table   Dorothy Parker (lower left) surrounded by
Robert Benchley, Alfred Lunt and Lynn Fontanne, Frank Crowninshield,
Alexander Woollcott, Heywood Broun, Marc Connelly, Frank Case, Franklin
P. Adams, Edna Ferber, George Kaufman and Robert Sherwood. Illustration
by Al Hirschfeld.

Anthem for Doomed Youth

What passing-bells for these who die as cattle?
  – Only the monstrous anger of the guns.
  Only the stuttering rifles' rapid rattle
Can patter out their hasty orisons.
No mockeries now for them; no prayers nor bells;
  Nor any voice of mourning save the choirs, –
The shrill demented choirs of wailing shells;
  And bugles calling for them from sad shires.

What candles may be held to speed them all?
  Not in the hands of boys, but in their eyes
Shall shine the holy glimmers of goodbyes.
  The pallor of girls' brows shall be their pall;
Their flowers the tenderness of patient minds,
And each slow dusk a drawing-down of blinds.

WILFRED OWEN (1893–1918)

What passing-bells for these who die as cattle?
  – Only the monstrous anger of the guns.
  Only the stuttering rifles' rapid rattle
Can patter out their hasty orisons.
No {music for all them, nor / mockeries for them from} prayers nor or bells
  Nor any voice of mourning save the choirs,
The shrill demented choirs of wailing shells;
  And bugles calling sad across the for them from sad shires.

What candles may be held to speed them all?
  Not in the hands of boys, but in their eyes
Shall shine the holy glimmers of goodbyes.
And The pallor of girls' brows shall be their pall;
  Their flowers the tenderness of silent minds,
  And each slow dusk a drawing-down of blinds.

Anthem for Doomed Youth   The pencilled corrections are by Siegfried
Sassoon, Owen's friend and fellow poet. BL Add. MS 43720, f.17.
By permission of The British Library Board.

A Picture*

for Tiantian's fifth birthday

Morning arrives in a sleeveless dress
apples tumble all over the earth
my daughter is drawing a picture
how vast is a five-year-old sky
your name has two windows
one opens towards a sun with no clock-hands
the other opens towards your father
who has become a hedgehog in exile
taking with him a few unintelligible characters
and a bright red apple
he has left your painting
how vast is a five-year-old sky

BEI DAO (b. 1949)

translated by BONNIE S. McDOUGALL

and CHEN MAIPING

*Tiantian, the nickname given to the poet's daughter, is written with two characters which look like a pair of windows. The same character also forms a part of the character for the word 'picture'.

穷无袖连
忘祝的不
暑到末大
地四公洗
动美莱束

A Picture   The first two lines of the original poem. Calligraphy by Yukki Yaura, © Yukki Yaura 1993 by permission of the artist.

Idyll

Not knowing even that we're on the way,
Until suddenly we're there. How shall we know?

There will be blackbirds, in a late March evening,
Blur of woodsmoke, whisky in grand glasses,

A poem of yours, waiting to be read; and one of mine;
A reflective bitch, a cat materialised

On a knee. All fears of present and future
Will be over, all guilts forgiven.

Maybe, heaven. Or maybe
We can get so far in this world. I'll believe we can.

U. A. FANTHORPE (b. 1929)

'Gray goose and gander'

Gray goose and gander,
　Waft your wings together,
And carry the good king's daughter
　Over the one strand river.

ANON. (date unknown)

Sonnet: On His Blindness

When I consider how my light is spent,
   Ere half my days, in this dark world and wide,
   And that one talent which is death to hide,
   Lodged with me useless, though my soul more bent
To serve therewith my maker, and present
   My true account, lest he returning chide,
   Doth God exact day-labour, light denied?
   I fondly ask; but Patience to prevent
That murmur, soon replies, God doth not need
   Either man's work or his own gifts, who best
   Bear his mild yoke, they serve him best, his state
Is kingly. Thousands at his bidding speed
   And post o'er land and ocean without rest:
   They also serve who only stand and wait.

JOHN MILTON (1608–74)

He wishes for the Cloths of Heaven

Had I the heavens' embroidered cloths,
Enwrought with golden and silver light,
The blue and the dim and the dark cloths
Of night and light and the half-light,
I would spread the cloths under your feet:
But I, being poor, have only my dreams;
I have spread my dreams under your feet;
Tread softly because you tread on my dreams.

W. B. YEATS (1865–1939)

Late Summer Fires

The paddocks shave black
with a foam of smoke that stays,
welling out of red-black wounds.

In the white of a drought
this happens. The hardcourt game.
Logs that fume are mostly cattle,

inverted, stubby. Tree stumps are kilns.
Walloped, wiped, hand-pumped,
even this day rolls over, slowly.

At dusk, a family drives sheep
out through the yellow
of the Aboriginal flag.

LES MURRAY (b. 1938)

Love in a Bathtub

Years later we'll remember the bathtub,
the position
            of the taps
the water, slippery
as if a bucketful
            of eels had joined us . . .
we'll be old, our children grown up
but we'll remember the water
                        sloshing out
the useless soap,
the mountain of wet towels.
'Remember the bathtub in Belfast?'
we'll prod each other –

SUJATA BHATT (b. 1956)

The Twa Corbies

As I was walking all alane,
I heard twa corbies making a mane;
The tane unto the tither say,
'Whar sall we gang and dine the day?'

'In behint yon auld fail dyke,
I wot there lies a new-slain knight;
And naebody kens that he lies there,
But his hawk, his hound, and lady fair.

'His hound is to the hunting gane,
His hawk to fetch the wild-fowl hame,
His lady's ta'en another mate,
Sae we may mak our dinner sweet.

'Ye'll sit on his white hause-bane,
And I'll pike out his bonnie blue een:
Wi' ae lock o' his gowden hair
We'll theek our nest when it grows bare.

'Mony a one for him makes mane,
But nane sall ken whar he is gane;
O'er his white banes, when they are bare,
The wind sall blaw for evermair.'

ANON (before 1800)

corbie: *raven*   mane: *moan*   hause-bane: *neck-bone*

The Great Frost

O roving Muse, recall that wondrous year,
When winter reigned in bleak Britannia's air;
When hoary Thames, with frosted osiers crowned,
Was three long moons in icy fetters bound.
The waterman, forlorn along the shore,
Pensive reclines upon his useless oar,
Sees harnessed steeds desert the stony town,
And wander roads unstable, not their own;
Wheels o'er the hardened waters smoothly glide,
And rase with whitened tracks the slippery tide.
Here the fat cook piles high the blazing fire,
And scarce the spit can turn the steer entire.
Booths sudden hide the Thames, long streets appear,
And numerous games proclaim the crowded fair.

from TRIVIA,
OR THE ART OF WALKING THE STREETS OF LONDON

JOHN GAY (1685–1732)

If I Could Tell You

Time will say nothing but I told you so,
Time only knows the price we have to pay;
If I could tell you I would let you know.

If we should weep when clowns put on their show,
If we should stumble when musicians play,
Time will say nothing but I told you so.

There are no fortunes to be told, although,
Because I love you more than I can say,
If I could tell you I would let you know.

The winds must come from somewhere when they blow,
There must be reasons why the leaves decay;
Time will say nothing but I told you so.

Perhaps the roses really want to grow,
The vision seriously intends to stay;
If I could tell you I would let you know.

Suppose the lions all get up and go,
And all the brooks and soldiers run away;
Will Time say nothing but I told you so?
If I could tell you I would let you know.

W.H. AUDEN (1907–73)

Spacetime

When I grow up and you get small,
then –

(In Kaluza's theory the fifth dimension
is represented as a circle
associated with every point
in spacetime)

– then when I die, I'll never be alive again?
                Never.
Never never?
                Never never.
Yes, but never never never?
                No . . . not never never never,
                just never never.

So we made
a small family contribution
to the quantum problem of eleven-dimensional
   supergravity.

MIROSLAV HOLUB (b. 1923)
translated by DAVID YOUNG and DANA HÁBOVÁ

Sun a-shine, rain a-fall

Sun a-shine an' rain a-fall,
The Devil an' him wife cyan 'gree at all,
The two o' them want one fish-head,
The Devil call him wife bonehead,
She hiss her teeth, call him cock-eye,
Greedy, worthless an' workshy,
While them busy callin' name,
The puss walk in, sey is a shame
To see a nice fish go to was'e,
Lef' with a big grin pon him face.

VALERIE BLOOM (b. 1956)

Sun a-shine, rain a-fall   Illustration by Michael Charlton.

Sonnet 18

Shall I compare thee to a summer's day?
Thou art more lovely and more temperate:
Rough winds do shake the darling buds of May,
And summer's lease hath all too short a date:
Sometime too hot the eye of heaven shines,
And often is his gold complexion dimmed;
And every fair from fair sometime declines,
By chance, or nature's changing course, untrimmed;
But thy eternal summer shall not fade,
Nor lose possession of that fair thou owest,
Nor shall death brag thou wander'st in his shade,
When in eternal lines to time thou growest;
    So long as men can breathe, or eyes can see,
    So long lives this, and this gives life to thee.

WILLIAM SHAKESPEARE (1564–1616)

A True and Faithful Inventory
of the Goods *belonging* to Dr. Swift, Vicar of
Lara Cor;

upon lending his House to the Bishop of Meath,
until his own was built

An Oaken, broken, Elbow-Chair;
A Cawdle-Cup, without an Ear;
A batter'd, shatter'd Ash Bedstead;
A Box of Deal, without a Lid;
A Pair of Tongs, but out of Joint;
A Back-Sword Poker, without Point;
A Pot that's crack'd across, around,
With an old knotted Garter bound;
an iron lock, without a Key;
A Wig, with hanging, quite grown grey;
A Curtain worn to Half a Stripe;
A Pair of Bellows, without Pipe;
A Dish, which might good Meat afford once;
An *Ovid*, and an old *Concordance*;
A Bottle Bottom, Wooden Platter,
One is for Meal, and one for Water:
There likewise is a Copper Skillet,
Which runs as fast out as you fill it;
A Candlestick, Snuff dish, and Save-all,
And thus his Household Goods you have all.
These, to your Lordship, as a Friend,
Till you have built, I freely lend:
They'll save your Lordship for a Shift;
Why not, as well as Doctor *Swift*?

THOMAS SHERIDAN (1687–1738)

Swineherd

When all this is over, said the swineherd,
I mean to retire, where
Nobody will have heard about my special skills
And conversation is mainly about the weather.

I intend to learn how to make coffee, at least as well
As the Portuguese lay-sister in the kitchen
And polish the brass fenders every day.
I want to lie awake at night
Listening to cream crawling to the top of the jug
And the water lying soft in the cistern.

I want to see an orchard where the trees grow in straight lines
And the yellow fox finds shelter between the navy-blue trunks,
Where it gets dark early in summer
And the apple-blossom is allowed to wither on the bough.

EILÉAN NÍ CHUILLEANÁIN (b. 1942)

'The world is too much with us'

The world is too much with us; late and soon,
Getting and spending, we lay waste our powers:
Little we see in nature that is ours;
We have given our hearts away, a sordid boon!
This Sea that bares her bosom to the moon;
The Winds that will be howling at all hours
And are up-gathered now like sleeping flowers;
For this, for every thing, we are out of tune;
It moves us not. Great God! I'd rather be
A Pagan suckled in a creed outworn;
So might I, standing on this pleasant lea,
Have glimpses that would make me less forlorn;
Have sight of Proteus coming from the sea;
Or hear old Triton blow his wreathed horn.

WILLIAM WORDSWORTH (1770–1850)

The world is too much with us; late and soon
Getting and spending we lay waste our powers
Little we see in nature that is ours;
We have given our hearts away, a sordid boon:
This sea that bares her bosom to the moon
The winds that will be howling at all hours,
And are upgather'd now like sleeping flowers,
For this, for every thing we are out of tune:
It moves us not. Great God! I'd rather be
A Pagan suckled in a creed outworn
So might I, standing on this pleasant lea
Have glimpses that would make me less
Have sight of Proteus coming from the sea forlorn
Or hear old Triton blow his wreathed horn.

From DC MS 44, a homemade notebook of Wordsworth's then
unpublished work, copied by his sister Dorothy and his wife Mary, for
Coleridge to take with him on a visit to Malta in 1804. The hand on this
poem is Dorothy Wordsworth's; the overlaid word 'hearts' is written by
William Wordsworth. DC MS 44 is one of the most important sources of
Wordsworth's early work. Reprinted by permission of the Wordsworth
Trust.

A Birthday

My heart is like a singing bird
   Whose nest is in a watered shoot;
My heart is like an apple-tree
   Whose boughs are bent with thick-set fruit;
My heart is like a rainbow shell
   That paddles in a halcyon sea;
My heart is gladder than all these
   Because my love is come to me.

Raise me a dais of silk and down;
   Hang it with vair and purple dyes;
Carve it in doves and pomegranates,
   And peacocks with a hundred eyes;
Work it in gold and silver grapes,
   In leaves and silver fleurs-de-lys;
Because the birthday of my life
   Is come, my love is come to me.

CHRISTINA ROSSETTI (1830–94)

Disillusionment of Ten O'Clock

The houses are haunted
By white night-gowns.
None are green,
Or purple with green rings,
Or green with yellow rings,
Or yellow with blue rings.
None of them are strange,
With socks of lace
And beaded ceintures.
People are not going
To dream of baboons and periwinkles.
Only, here and there, an old sailor,
Drunk and asleep in his boots,
Catches tigers
In red weather.

WALLACE STEVENS (1879–1955)

The Boundary Commission

You remember that village where the border ran
Down the middle of the street,
With the butcher and baker in different states?
Today he remarked how a shower of rain

Had stopped so cleanly across Golightly's lane
It might have been a wall of glass
That had toppled over. He stood there, for ages,
To wonder which side, if any, he should be on.

PAUL MULDOON (b. 1951)

Arrival 1946

The boat docked in at Liverpool.
From the train Tariq stared
at an unbroken line of washing
from the North West to Euston.

These are strange people, he thought –
an Empire, and all this washing,
the underwear, the Englishman's garden.
It was Monday, and very sharp.

MONIZA ALVI (b. 1954)

NOTES TO THE POEMS

page 25 **Up in the Morning Early**   'The chorus of this song is old; the two stanzas are mine' (Burns's note).

33 **The Trees**   Philip Larkin was on the Compton Poetry Fund committee when it approved a grant which enabled us to pay for the first year of advertising spaces on the Underground. He took a special interest in the project and wrote to us with useful suggestions: 'I have always liked the Wayside Pulpit placards (''Don't Put Your Wishbone Where Your Backbone Ought To Be''), and think it might be equally inspiring to be able to read on a tube journey poems that served as a reminder that the world of the imagination existed . . . What level of appreciation are you aiming at? Somerset Maugham, in his play-writing days, said that if you saw the audiences' taste in terms of the alphabet, it was best to aim at letter O. I don't think it would hurt to remind people of poems they already know; not everyone will know them.' Shortly before his death, he wrote to us again: 'I am glad your project is being favourably regarded; it makes me wonder whether I shall ever actually see one of the poems in the proposed location.' Sadly, he died before the first set of poems was posted.

35 **The Sick Rose**   William Blake, known in his own day as an engraver rather than a poet, published his *Songs of Innocence* and *Songs of Experience* in hand-engraved, hand-coloured editions of his own design ('illuminated printing'). This meant, in effect, that the poems remained virtually unknown until Blake was rediscovered as a great visionary poet in the 1860s. Both 'The Sick Rose' and 'The Tyger' were published in *Songs of Experience* (1794).

37 **At Lord's**   Cricket's laureate is Francis Thompson, whose 'At Lord's' evokes the image of an exiled Lancastrian watching a match at Lord' cricket ground but seeing in his mind's eye a game played elsewhere many years before. The poem is a reduced version of a longer poer which mentions, as well as the Lancashire batsmen Hornby an

Barlow, Gloucestershire's 'resistless' Grace brothers. When the poster appeared on the Tube, the former cricketer Mike Selvey reprinted it in full in his *Guardian* Cricket Diary ('No, this isn't the arts page – just a bit of our cultural heritage for a change') and we were inundated with requests for the poem, mostly from Lancashire.

41   **Composed Upon Westminster Bridge**   'Written on the roof of a coach, on my way to France' (Wordsworth's note). With Wordsworth's dating of the poem in mind, we arranged a 'workshop' on Westminster Bridge at dawn on 3 September 1986. We advertised in the London listings magazines and to our amazement between twenty and thirty people turned up, including a visiting American professor and the poet Wendy Cope. At dawn (twelve minutes past six, BST) we read the poem aloud. Then we settled down to watch the sun rise and write some poems of our own. Aware that the Thames crosses England from west to east, we gazed downstream, waiting to see the sun. We might have waited a very long time, as on this stretch the Thames runs due north (towards Islington, York and the Arctic circle). In any case, it was an overcast morning. When the sun suddenly gleamed through, apparently to our south, were were mightily surprised. Once we were cold enough, we adjourned to a local coffee shop to warm up and read our poems.

When T. S. Eliot's 'Prelude' was displayed on the Tube, we held a second 'winter' workshop at dusk on Waterloo Bridge, somewhat impeded by rain and sleet.

3   **The Loch Ness Monster's Song**   The author explained in conversation that the lonely monster rises from the loch and looks round for the companions of his youth – prehistoric reptiles – and, finding nobody he knows, he descends again to the depths after a brief swearing session. This was confirmed by a nine-year-old boy in a workshop, who said the monster was 'looking for a diplodocus'. When asked how he knew that, he said, 'It says so.' It does.

Some years ago, Edwin Morgan was commissioned by the Scottish Arts Council to write a series of poems for the inauguration of Glasgow's refurbished Underground system. He sent us this sample, which sent such alarm through the Strathclyde transport executive that they decided against using the poems.

The Subway Piranhas

Did anyone tell you
that in each subway train
there is one special seat
with a small hole in it
and underneath the seat
is a tank of piranha-fish
which have not been fed
for quite some time.
The fish become agitated
by the shoogling of the train
and jump up through the seat.
The resulting skeletons
of unlucky passengers
turn an honest penny
for the transport executive,
hanging far and wide
in medical schools.

44 **Living** On learning that a poem of hers was to appear on the Underground, Denise Levertov, who was born in London but has lived mainly in the United States, wrote to us: 'I am totally thrilled at the idea of having a poem in the Tube. I spent innumerable hours in the Tube from age 12–23, and a good many before and since, too. I am in fact a sort of Tube Rat, like a "rat" of the Paris Opera – a *denizen*. Appearance in American trains and buses means little to me – but London, ah, London! – that's different.'

49 **I Am Becoming My Mother** The title poem of a volume for which Lorna Goodison was awarded the Commonwealth Poetry Prize (Americas region) for 1986.

50 **'Tagus farewell'** Written in June 1539 in Spain, where Wyatt was Ambassador at the court of Charles V. Wyatt had just been recalled to London by Henry VIII, and the last lines of the poem may reflect some uneasiness at the fate awaiting him at home. The Spanish and Portuguese River Tagus is famous for its gold. Brutus, a descendant of Aeneas, dreamed that he was destined to found a kingdom in Albion.

53 **Lines** *from* **Endymion**   The famous opening lines of a long poem, and the first of a number of extracts in our collection.

54 **Goodbye**   Charlie Parker was an American jazz saxophonist, possibly the greatest of them all, who died in 1955, aged thirty-four.

57 **'So we'll go no more a-roving'**   Written in a letter to Thomas Moore in which Byron admits to over-indulging in carnival festivities: 'The mumming closed with a masked ball at the Fenice, where I went, as also to most of the ridottos, etc., etc., and, though I did not dissipate much upon the whole, yet I find "the sword wearing out the scabbard", though I have but just turned the corner of twenty-nine.'

71 **The Coming of Grendel**   Another extract. In this passage from the Old English epic, the monster Grendel (the original inhabitant of the land) closes in on the glittering wine-hall of the colonisers, where he means to wreak terrible havoc. The translation tries to be as literal as possible, while keeping the linguistic feeling of the original, with its resounding alliteration.

73 **Sonnet from the Portuguese**   The sonnets have no Portuguese original; they were written in secret the year before the poet's marriage to Robert Browning and tell the story of their unfolding love. In a letter to Leigh Hunt, Robert Browning explained how he persuaded Elizabeth Barrett Browning to publish these intimate poems: 'I never suspected the existence of those "Sonnets from the Portuguese" till three years after they were written. They were shown to me in consequence of some word of mine, just as they had been suppressed through some mistaken word; it was I who would not bear that sacrifice, and thought of the subterfuge of a name.' The sequence of forty-three sonnets appears as the final work in *Poems of Elizabeth Barrett Browning* (1850), immediately preceded by 'Catarina to Camoens' – a love poem addressed by his dying mistress to the great sixteenth-century Portuguese poet. The suggestion is that 'Catarina' may have written the Sonnets as well, though this is not said explicitly – and the poems quickly became among the most celebrated love poems in the English language.

Symphony in Yellow   The sketch of Wilde was formerly attributed to Whistler, rather than to his wife Beatrice. They were friends and neighbours of Wilde's in Tite Street, Chelsea.

---

79 **'Sumer is icumen in'** Robert Graves and Laura Riding comment in their paper 'On Anthologies': 'Every possible polite explanation is given in popular anthologies for *verteth* to distract attention from the poetic meaning that the buck, full of Spring grass, *farteth*, i.e. breaks wind.' Scholarly debate still rages on this question, but on balance we agree with Graves and Riding, and have emended our earlier version.

90 **Roundel** *from* **The Parliament of Fowls** Sung by the assembled birds at the end of the St Valentine's Day festivities, when each bird has been happily paired off with its mate. 'The note,' the narrator explains, 'imaked was in France' – home of courtly love, which Chaucer's delicious poem gently parodies.

95 *from* **To the City of London** The fourth stanza of a seven-stanza 'balade' recited during Christmas week, 1501, at a dinner held by the Lord Mayor in honour of the visiting Scottish Ambassador. Usually assumed to be the work of the Scottish poet William Dunbar, who was in London at the time.

96 **On First Looking into Chapman's Homer** Composed during October 1816, at dawn, as Keats walked home to Southwark from Clerkenwell, where he had been visiting his former schoolteacher Charles Cowden Clarke. They had stayed up all night reading Homer in the magnificent translation of George Chapman.

100 **'I have a gentil cock'** We have retained the old spelling of 'gentil' to suggest 'gently bred' or 'aristocratic'. Chanticleer, in Chaucer's *Nun's Priest's Tale*, is another 'gentil cock', described in similar terms:

> His coomb was redder than the fyn coral,
> And batailled as it were a castel wal;
> His byle was blak, and as the jeet it shoon,
> Lyk asure were his legges and his toon,
> His nayles whitter than the lylye flour,
> And lyk the burned gold was his colour.

(lines 39–44)

103 **Mmenson** *mmenson:* an orchestra of seven elephant tusk horns used

on state occasions to relate history; *Agades*: a town in the western Sudan; *Sokoto*: a town in what is now northern Nigeria. (Notes by the author.)

04 **Light** Diane Wakoski felt that the extract from 'The Hitchhikers' which originally appeared on the Underground would represent a distortion of the poem if reproduced in a book, and we were happy to substitute this complete short poem.

06 **'You took away all the oceans and all the room'** In 1934, after he was discovered to be the author of a bitter satire on Stalin, Mandelstam was arrested and exiled for three years, first to a small town in the Urals, then to the provincial town of Voronezh, where this poem was written. He was rearrested in 1938, and died en route to a labour camp.

10 **Old English Riddle** Suggested answer: *Bookworm*. This reminds us that bookworms have always been a genuine problem to book owners. This charming riddle is No. 47 in *The Exeter Book*, probably transcribed c. 960–70 and later owned by the first Bishop of Exeter. The riddles vary greatly in subject and style. Many are about the animal kingdom, others are about artefacts and yet others about the forces of nature – and there is a sprinkling of teasing double entendre, of a type still popular, which leads the reader to imagine two parallel solutions, one obscene, the other innocent.

8 **The Cries of London** Two stanzas of a broadside ballad in the 'Roxburghe Ballads', a unique collection of songs and ballads printed between 1560 and 1700, collected by Robert, Earl of Oxford, and now in the British Library. The 'cries' can be heard to this day in many traditional London markets.

'Ich am of Irlonde' Fragment of a medieval carol, written with other rhymes and doggerel in French and English on a single vellum leaf, now in the Bodleian Library, Oxford. W. B. Yeats uses the lines as a refrain for 'I am of Ireland', in *Words for Music Perhaps*:

> *'I am of Ireland,*
> *And the Holy Land of Ireland,*
> *And time runs on,' cried she.*
> *'Come out of charity,*
> *Come dance with me in Ireland.'*

126 **"The Uncertainty of the Poet"** 'The Tate Gallery yesterday announced that it had paid £1 million for a Giorgio de Chirico master-piece, The Uncertainty of the Poet. It depicts a torso and a bunch of bananas' – *Guardian*, 2 April 1985. *With a Poet's Eye: A Tate Gallery Anthology*, for which the poem was first commissioned, presents paint-ings and poems side by side.

127 **'I saw a Peacock with a fiery tail'** In his anthology *Come Hither* (1923), Walter de la Mare comments: 'So may the omission of a few commas effect a wonder in the imagination.' The first printing we were able to find was in *Westminster Drollery, Or, A Choice Collection of the Newest Songs and Poems both at Court and Theaters*, by A Person of Quality (1671). There the verse is headed: 'These following are to be understood two ways', and commas half-way through each line encourage the reader to pick up the double meaning. We have followed later editors in omitting the commas.

130 **On Himself** The poet has been profoundly deaf since the age of seven, following an attack of scarlet fever. This poem appeared on the Underground in September 1991. A 1992 collection of David Wright's poems includes these moving lines:

An Appearance of Success

Some verses, written when he was alive,
A poster broadcast on the Underground;
My life (an actor plays him) televised;
Fame of a kind, if not recognition;
Pleasing enough but not enough to please
An unambitiousness at seventy-one,
Or pierce the unawareness of the dead:
This present I'd have loved to give to him
To make amends,
– My father – an appearance of success
In his deaf difficult son;
Something to recompense
As may have seemed to him
Rewardless and too long a sacrifice.

132 **The Passionate Shepherd to his Love** Because of limited space, in our Underground poster we adapted the four-stanza version published in *The Passionate Pilgrim* (1599). The six-stanza version published in *England's Helicon* (1600) has been reprinted ever since in this form, often with its companion piece, 'The Nymph's Reply to the Shepherd' by Sir Walter Raleigh:

> If all the world and love were young,
> And truth in every shepherd's tongue,
> These pretty pleasures might me move
> To live with thee and be thy love.
>
> Time drives the flocks from field to fold,
> When rivers rage and rocks grow cold,
> And Philomel becometh dumb;
> The rest complains of cares to come.
>
> The flowers do fade, and wanton fields
> To wayward winter reckoning yields;
> A honey tongue, a heart of gall,
> Is fancy's spring, but sorrow's fall.
>
> Thy gowns, thy shoes, thy beds of roses,
> Thy cap, thy kirtle, and thy posies
> Soon break, soon wither, soon forgotten, –
> In folly ripe, in reason rotten.
>
> Thy belt of straw and ivy buds,
> Thy coral clasps, and amber studs,
> All these in me no means can move
> To come to thee and be thy love.
>
> But could youth last and love still breed,
> Had joys no date nor age no need,
> Then these delights my mind might move
> To live with thee and be thy love.

33 **Letter to André Billy** During the First World War, Apollinaire served in the French artillery and infantry. He survived a skull wound towards the end of the war, but died a few months later in the influenza

epidemic ravaging Paris. In a letter to his friend André Billy, he wrote of his *Calligrammes*: 'They are an idealization of *vers-libre* poetry and of typographical precision at a time when typography is brilliantly ending its career, at the dawn of new methods of reproduction, the cinema and the gramophone.' In the original French text, typography is used to suggest the shape of a bird of prey (as a shell), an eye, and a cathedral (specifically, Notre Dame).

Poème epistolaire

Premier canonnier conducteur
Je suis au front et te salue
Non non tu n'as pas la berlue
Cinquante-neuf est mon secteur

J'entends siff$_l$$_e$$_r$ l'oiseau
Le
bel oiseau rap^a^{c}$_e$

Je vo^i^{s} de lo$_i$$_n$
La cathédrale

```
        O    C
        M    H
        O    E
        N  A  R
        N  D  R  E
        B I L L Y
```

139 **To Emilia V –**   Mary Shelley discovered these lines after Shelley's death in one of his notebooks, when she was transcribing his poems for publication. The manuscript draft which we reproduce, the only known source of the poem, was composed at the same time as the opening lines of *Epipsychidion*, Shelley's celebration of love. The same images appear in both texts: music, memory, rose leaves (or petals).

> Sweet Spirit! Sister of that orphan one,
> Whose empire is the name thou weepest on,
> In my heart's temple I suspend to thee
> These votive wreaths of withered memory.

Poor captive bird! who, from thy narrow cage,
Pourest such music, that it might assuage
The rugged hearts of those who prisoned thee,
Were they not deaf to all sweet melody;
This song shall be thy rose: its petals pale
Are dead, indeed, my adored Nightingale!
But soft and fragrant is the faded blossom,
And it has no thorn left to wound thy bosom.

(1–12)

Teresa Emilia Viviani, to whom these lines were addressed, was the daughter of the Governor of Pisa. Shelley, who lived in Pisa in 1821–22, visited her in the convent where she was awaiting an arranged marriage, and he took a deep interest in her fate. She wrote sonnets and an essay on Love, a sentence of which Shelley uses as an epigraph to *Epipsychidion* ('Verses addressed to the noble and unfortunate lady, Emilia V –, now imprisoned in the convent of –'). 'Music, when soft voices die' also pays a compliment to Emilia's writing, the 'thoughts' which, when their author is gone, Love itself shall slumber on. Shelley's editors, following Mary Shelley, entitle the lines 'To –,' which we have expanded on the suggestion of the manuscript evidence.

142 **The Lobster Quadrille** From *Alice in Wonderland*. This poem, which parodies Mary Howitt's ' ''Will you walk into my Parlour?'' said the spider to the fly', is sung to Alice by the Mock Turtle, while he and his friend the Gryphon 'solemnly' dance on the sea-shore, a moment magically captured by Sir John Gielgud and Malcolm Muggeridge in Jonathan Miller's television version of *Alice*.

144 **I shall say what inordinate love is** 'Inordinate' rather than lawful love is the subject of this lyric. In the original MS, the poem is accompanied by a briefer Latin original (which also appears elsewhere). The Latin treats merely of *Amor* (love), rather than the inordinate variety:

Dicam quid sit Amor: Amor est insania mentis
Ardor inextinctus, insaciata fames
Dulce malum, mala dulcedo, dulcissimus error
Absque labore quies, absque quiete labor.

Of the many English variations on this theme during the Renaissance, probably the most famous is Shakespeare's defintion of 'lust' in Sonnet 129:

> Mad in pursuit, and in possession so;
> Had, having, and in quest to have, extreme;
> A bliss in proof, and proved, a very woe,
> Before, a joy proposed; behind, a dream.

145 **A red red Rose**   Burns copied out a slightly different version of this song in a letter to his friend Alexander Cunningham, describing it as 'a simple old Scots song' which he had picked up in the country. Virtually every stanza of the song can be matched in oral tradition and earlier broadsheet ballads, and Burns's editors disagree on the extent to which he may have altered or improved it. But the final version seems unmistakably to have his special touch, in its tenderness and lyricism and its impeccable rhythms.

148 **To Someone Who Insisted I Look Up Someone**   The Editors met the American poet X. J. Kennedy several years ago, and to our surprise he remembered us well. He wrote from Bedford, Massachusetts: 'What a gleeful thing, to have lines perused by London straphangers (or is it pole-clingers?). Your picking that item delighted me more than if the Swedish Academy had handed me the Nobel Prize, and seemed about equally incredible.'

149 **Two Fragments**   Sappho, the great lyric poet of the ancient world, called by Plato 'the Tenth Muse', was born in the late 7th century on the island of Lesbos. Much of her poetry has come to us from fragments of papyrus discovered in the late 19th century; other poems, including the two fragments translated here, were quoted by ancient grammarians.

150 **I Am**   Written in Northampton County Asylum, this is the best known of John Clare's many poems. After a brief period of fame as a 'peasant genius', Clare became more and more disorientated, and lived in mental asylums from 1837 until his death in 1864. The confusion from which he suffered did not affect his lucidity as a poet. He continued until the end to produce work of a high order.

151 **Dream Boogie** Langston Hughes, born in Joplin, Missouri, was a major figure in the Harlem Renaissance of the 1920s and '30s. 'Dream Boogie' is the first poem of *Montage of a Dream Deferred* (1951), a sequence of poems which use the idiom of bebop to portray the dreams of ordinary men and women in New York's Black ghetto.

155 **The Flaw in Paganism** Dorothy Parker, poet, journalist and short-story writer, was one of the inner circle of wits and literary celebrities who met regularly for lunch at the Algonquin Hotel in New York in the 1920s. She worked in Hollywood as a scriptwriter, became involved in radical politics, and was blacklisted during the McCarthy period.

Soon after this poem appeared on the Underground, we received a phone call from a vicar asking permission to reprint it in the *Church Times* – which would have amused the author.

156 **Anthem for Doomed Youth** 'Above all I am not concerned with Poetry. My subject is War, and the pity of War. The Poetry is in the pity' (from Wilfred Owen's draft *Preface* to his war poems). Owen's poetical manifesto has an added poignancy since he was killed in France just seven days before the Armistice. This sonnet contains a bitter parody on the paraphernalia of formal mourning.

158 **A Picture** Bei Dao ('North Island') is the pen name of Zhao Zhenkai, a leading Chinese dissident writer. He was in Berlin at the time of the Tiananmen Square massacre (4 June 1989), and has been unable since then to return to Beijing, where his wife and daughter live. 'A Picture' was written in 1990, during a six-month stay in Stockholm.

161 **Gray Goose and Gander** The origins of this charming fragment are unknown. Its first printing is in J. O. Halliwell's *Nursery Rhymes of England*, 3rd Edition (1844).

162 **Sonnet: On His Blindness** Milton went totally blind in his early forties. In another sonnet on his blindness, written for his friend and pupil Cyriack Skinner, Milton explains that he lost his sight 'In liberty's defence' – that is, through writing his anti-clerical and political pamphlets, including *Areopagitica*, his eloquent plea for freedom of thought and the press.

164   **Late Summer Fires**   The regeneration of the land by setting fire to it is an ancient Aboriginal technique which does not find favour with all modern Australians. Les Murray kindly wrote to us elucidating two phrases in the poem: 'The "hardcourt game" is life in Outback Australia, where soils tend to be pink to ochre to blood red and most often very hard and bare, under the cover of low bush . . . So your note could say "hardcourt: refers to the hard red soils of inland Australia." And the Aboriginal flag (black and red, with a yellow disc at the centre), relates to that – the red once again standing for that soil and the blood spilt on it, while the black's for the people and the yellow disc is the sun.'

166   **The Twa Corbies**   First printed in Sir Walter Scott, *Minstrelsy of the Scottish Border* (1802–3). Readers may like to compare the Scots border ballad with the popular English ballad, **The Three Ravens**, first set to music by Thomas Ravenscroft in 1611:

> There were three Ravens sat on a tree,
> > *Downe a downe, hay down, hay downe.*
> There were three Ravens sat on a tree,
> > *With a downe.*
> There were three Ravens sat on a tree,
> They were as blacke as they might be.
> > *With a downe derrie, derrie, derrie, downe, downe.*
>
> The one of them said to his mate,
> Where shall we our breakefast take?
>
> Downe in yonder greene field,
> There lies a Knight slain under his shield.
>
> His hounds they lie downe at his feete,
> So well they can their Master keepe.
>
> His Haukes they flie so eagerly,
> There's no fowle dare him come nie.
>
> Downe there comes a fallow Doe,
> As great with yong as she might goe.
>
> She lift up his bloudy hed,
> And kist his wounds that were so red.
>
> She got him up upon her backe,
> And carried him to earthen lake.

She buried him before the prime,
She was dead her selfe ere even-song time.

God send every gentleman
Such haukes, such hounds, and such a Leman.

167 **The Great Frost** 'Frost fairs' were held on the frozen Thames in the bitter winters of 1684 and 1698. John Evelyn described the extraordinary scene in his Diary, 24 January 1684: 'Coaches plied from Westminster to the Temple and from several other stairs to and fro, as in the streets, sleds, sliding with skates, a bull-baiting, horse and coach races, puppet plays and interludes, cooks, tippling and other lewd places, so that it seemed to be a Bacchanalian triumph, or carnival on the water.'

172 **A True and Faithful Inventory** Printed in *Swift: Poetical Works*, edited by Herbert Davis (OUP 1967). Thomas Sheridan was an Irish schoolmaster, one of several friends with whom Swift liked to exchange puns, riddles and verse epistles.

174 **Thanks Forever** A modern view of a scene similar to that described by Walt Whitman in 'Crossing Brooklyn Ferry', in which the poet stands at the ferry rail imagining later generations standing at the same spot, gazing at the same river and sky. The first section of Whitman's poem celebrating his beloved city was displayed on the London Underground, alongside 'Thanks Forever', as part of an exchange of poems with the New York City Transit Authority:

Flood-tide below me! I see you face to face!
Clouds of the west – sun there half an hour high – I see you
    also face to face.

Crowds of men and women attired in the usual costumes, how
    curious you are to me!
On the ferry boats, the hundreds and hundreds that cross,
    returning home, are more curious to me than you suppose,
And you that shall cross from shore to shore years hence are
    more to me, and more in my meditations, than you might
    suppose . . .

INDEX OF POETS
AND TRANSLATORS

INDEX OF FIRST LINES

THE EDITORS

Gerard Benson has worked as an actor, teacher, drama school and university lecturer. He is a member of The Barrow Poets, with whom he has toured extensively, and a *Times Educational Supplement* columnist. He is the editor of the award-winning Puffin anthology *This Poem Doesn't Rhyme*, and author of *The Magnificent Callisto* (Blackie) for 8–12 year olds.

Judith Chernaik was born in New York, but has lived in London since 1972. She has lectured at British and American universities, reviews for the *Times Literary Supplement* and other journals, and has written features and talks for the BBC. She is the author of *The Lyrics of Shelley* and four novels, most recently *Mab's Daughters*.

Cicely Herbert is a writer, a member of The Barrow Poets, and an adult education teacher. She has written several performance pieces with music by Jim Parker. These include, for BBC TV, *Petticoat Lane*, and two concert pieces commissioned by the Nash Ensemble, *Scenes from Victorian London* and *La Comédie Humaine*. Her poetry includes *In Hospital*, 1992.

A NOTE OF THANKS

'POEMS ON THE UNDERGROUND' could not have prospered without the continued help and cooperation of London Underground, which provides advertising spaces free of charge, and has assumed all production costs of the programme. We are also grateful for financial support from the Calouste Gulbenkian Foundation, the Stefan Zweig Programme of The British Library, and the British Council, which displays the Tube posters in its many libraries abroad. Support from publishers has come from Faber and Faber, Oxford University Press, Virago, W. W. Norton, Jonathan Cape, Century Hutchinson, Chatto and Windus, and Grafton Books. We have been particularly fortunate in our designers, and are grateful to Pentagram for providing the original design and to Tom Davidson, who has designed our posters since 1989.

The number of friends and colleagues who have generously given encouragement and practical advice is too great to list here – to all, our thanks.

Readers may like to know that copies of the Tube posters can be purchased from the London Transport Museum. Full details can be obtained by writing to Poems on the Underground, London Transport Museum, Freepost, Covent Garden, London WC2E 7BB. No stamp is required.